LAO-TZU'S TAOTECHING

BOOKS BY RED PINE

In Such Hard Times: The Poetry of Wei Ying-wu

Zen Baggage: A Pilgrimage to China

The Platform Sutra: The Zen Teaching of Hui-neng

The Heart Sutra: The Womb of Buddhas

Poems of the Masters: China's Classic Anthology of T'ang and Sung Dynasty Verse

The Diamond Sutra: The Perfection of Wisdom

The Collected Songs of Cold Mountain

The Zen Works of Stonehouse: Poems and Talks of a Fourteenth-Century Chinese Hermit

The Clouds Should Know Me by Now: Buddhist Poet Monks of China
   (co-edited with Mike O'Connor)

Guide to Capturing a Plum Blossom by Sung Po-jen

Road to Heaven: Encounters with Chinese Hermits

The Zen Teaching of Bodhidharma

P'u Ming's Oxherding Pictures and Verses

LAO-TZU's TAOTECHING

with selected commentaries from the past 2,000 years

translated by

RED PINE

Revised Edition

Copper Canyon Press
Port Townsend, Washington

Cover art: Peter de Lory, "Devil's Raceway," 1989.
Silver gelatin, 15 × 15 inches. www.peterdelory.com

Copper Canyon Press is in residence at Fort Worden State Park in
Port Townsend, Washington, under the auspices of Centrum. Centrum is a gathering
place for artists and creative thinkers from around the world, students of all ages and
backgrounds, and audiences seeking extraordinary cultural enrichment.

Acknowledgments: Work on this book would not have been completed without food
stamps and energy assistance from the Department of Social and Health Services and
Olympic Community Action Programs in Port Townsend, Washington.
I am indebted to them both.

LIBRARY OF CONGRESS CATALOGING-IN-PUBLICATION DATA
Laozi.
[Dao de jing. English]
Lao-tzu's Taoteching: with selected commentaries of the
past 2,000 years / translated by Red Pine. — Rev. 3rd ed.
p. cm.
English and Chinese.
ISBN 978-1-55659-290-4 (pbk.: alk. paper)
I. Red Pine, 1943–   II. Title.
BL1900.L26E5 2009C
299.5'1482 — dc22
2009020828

THIRD EDITION
7 9 8

COPPER CANYON PRESS
Post Office Box 271
Port Townsend, Washington 98368
www.coppercanyonpress.org

for Ku Lien-chang

CONTENTS

———

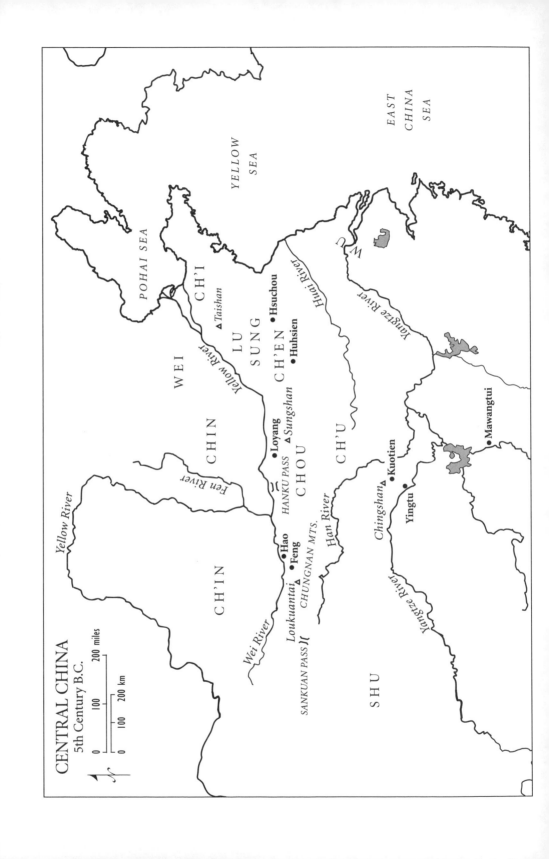

CENTRAL CHINA
5th Century B.C.

0   100   200 miles
0   100   200 km

POHAI SEA

YELLOW SEA

EAST CHINA SEA

CH'I

WEI

LU

SUNG

▲Taishan

•Hsuchou

CH'EN

•Huhsien

Yellow River

CHIN

▲Sungshan

•Loyang

CHOU

HANKU PASS

Fen River

Yellow River

Wei River

•Hao
•Feng

Loukuantai▲

CHUNGNAN MTS.

SANKUAN PASS){

CH'IN

SHU

Han River

CH'U

Chingshan▲

•Kuotien

•Yingtu

Yangtze River

Huai River

Yangtze River

•Mawangtui

PREFACE TO THE REVISED EDITION

Since my translation of the *Taoteching* was first published in 1996, I have looked at it from time to time, and not only to track down a reference. Sometimes I have wondered why I translated something a certain way and if another rendering would not have been better. I am glad for any opportunity to revisit an earlier effort. In this case, the opportunity was provided by the discovery of another set of early copies of the text.

In 1993, three bundles of thin bamboo slats containing selections of *Tao-teching* verses were unearthed in a tomb near the village of Kuotien/Guodian in Hupei province. The tomb belonged to the tutor of the crown prince of the ancient state of Ch'u, and the bundles were probably used for different levels of instruction. Since these newly discovered copies have been dated to 300 B.C., give or take a decade or two, they constitute by far our earliest version of the *Tao-teching*, a hundred years earlier than those found at Mawangtui. However, unlike the Mawangtui copies, the Kuotien copies only include selections. They don't include the entire eighty-one-verse text, and they rarely include the entire text of the verses they quote. Sometimes, they quote no more than a line or two. Of course, it remains a point of contention, which I prefer not to address, whether they were part of a proto-*Taoteching* or whether they were merely selections from an already complete text. Still, their discovery has given us a whole new set of variants to consider. And they have given me the excuse to review what I liked about my previous translation and what I didn't like. No doubt, I will be just as ready to revisit this work again the next time another early copy is unearthed.

Red Pine
Autumn at the Gate, Year of the Ox
Port Townsend, Washington

INTRODUCTION TO THE 1996 EDITION

The *Taoteching* is at heart a simple book. Written at the end of the sixth century B.C. by a man called Lao-tzu, it's a vision of what our lives would be like if we were more like the dark, new moon.

Lao-tzu teaches us that the dark can always become light and contains within itself the potential for growth and long life, while the light can only become dark and brings with it decay and early death. Lao-tzu chose long life. Thus, he chose the dark.

The word that Lao-tzu chose to represent this vision was *Tao,* 道. But *tao* means "road" or "way" and doesn't appear to have anything to do with darkness. The character is made up of two graphs: 首 (head) and 辶 (go). To make sense of how the character came to be constructed, early Chinese philologists concluded that "head" must mean the start of something and that the two graphs together show someone starting on a trip. But I find the explanation of a modern scholar of comparative religion, Tu Er-wei, more convincing. Professor Tu says the "head" in the character *tao* is the face of the moon. And the meaning of "road" comes from watching this disembodied face as it moves across the sky.

Professor Tu also notes that *tao* shares a common linguistic heritage with words that mean "moon" or "new moon" in other cultures: Tibetans call the moon *da-ua;* the Miao, who now live in southwest China but who lived in the same state as Lao-tzu when he was alive, call it *tao-tie;* the ancient Egyptians called it *thoth.* Tu Er-wei could have added *dar-sha,* which means "new moon" in Sanskrit.

However, the heart of Tu's thesis is not linguistic but textual, and based on references within the *Taoteching.* Lao-tzu says the Tao is between Heaven and Earth, it's Heaven's Gate, it's empty but inexhaustible, it doesn't die, it waxes and wanes, it's distant and dark, it doesn't try to be full, it's the light that doesn't blind, it has thirty spokes and two thirteen-day (visible) phases, it can be strung like a bow or expand and contract like a bellows, it moves the other way (relative to the sun, it appears/rises later and later), it's the great image, the hidden immortal, the crescent soul, the dark union, the dark womb, the dark beyond dark. If this isn't the moon, what is it?

Tu Er-wei has, I think, uncovered a deep and primitive layer of the *Taoteching* that has escaped the attention of other scholars. Of course, we cannot say for certain that Lao-tzu was consciously aware of the Tao's association with the moon. But we have his images, and they are too often lunar to dismiss as accidental.

In associating the Tao with the moon, Lao-tzu was not alone. The symbol Taoists have used since ancient times to represent the Tao, ☯, shows the two conjoined phases of the moon. And how could they ignore such an obvious connection between its cycle of change and our own? Every month we watch the moon grow from nothing to a luminous disk that scatters the stars and pulls the tides within us all. The oceans feel it. The earth feels it. Plants and animals feel it. Humans also feel it, though it is women who seem to be most aware of it. In the *Huangti Neiching,* or *Yellow Emperor's Internal Book of Medicine,* Ch'i Po explained this to the Yellow Emperor, "When the moon begins to grow, blood and breath begin to surge. When the moon is completely full, blood and breath are at their fullest, tendons and muscles are at their strongest. When the moon is completely empty, tendons and muscles are at their weakest" (8.26).

The advance of civilization has separated us from this easy lunar awareness. We call people affected by the moon "lunatics," making clear our disdain for its power. Lao-tzu redirects our vision to this ancient mirror. But instead of pointing to its light, he points to its darkness. Every month the moon effortlessly shows us that something comes from nothing. Lao-tzu asks us to emulate this aspect of the moon—not the full moon, which is destined to wane, but the new moon, which holds the promise of rebirth. And while he has us gazing at the moon's dark mirror, he asks why we don't live longer than we do. After all, don't we share the same nature as the moon? And isn't the moon immortal?

Scholars tend to ignore Lao-tzu's emphasis on darkness and immortality, for it takes the book beyond the reach of academic analysis. For scholars, darkness is just a more poetic way of describing the mysterious. And immortality is a euphemism for long life. Over the years, they have distilled what they call Lao-tzu's "Taoist philosophy" from the later developments of "Taoist religion." They call the *Taoteching* a treatise on political or military strategy, or they see it as primitive scientific naturalism or utopianism—or just a bunch of sayings.

But trying to force the *Taoteching* into the categories of modern discourse not only distorts the *Taoteching* but also treats the traditions that later Taoists have associated with the text as irrelevant and misguided. Meanwhile, the *Taoteching* continues to inspire millions of Chinese as a spiritual text. And I have tried to present it in that dark light. The words of philosophers fail here. If words are of any use at all, they are the words of the poet. For poetry has the ability to point us toward the truth then stand aside, while prose stands in the doorway relating all the wonders on the other side but rarely lets us pass.

In this respect, the *Taoteching* is unique among the great literary works of the Chou dynasty (1122–221 B.C.). Aside from the anonymous poems and folksongs of the *Shihching*, or *Book of Odes,* we have no other poetic work from this early period of Chinese history. The wisdom of other sages was conveyed in prose. Although I haven't attempted to reproduce Lao-tzu's poetic devices (Hsu Yung-chang identifies twenty-eight different kinds of rhyme), I have tried to convey the poetic feel with which he strings together images for our breath and spirit, but not necessarily our minds. For the *Taoteching* is one long poem written in praise of something we cannot name, much less imagine.

Despite the elusiveness and namelessness of the Tao, Lao-tzu tells us we can approach it through *Te. Te* means "virtue," in the sense of "moral character" as well as "power to act." Yen Ling-feng says, "Virtue is the manifestation of the Way. The Way is what Virtue contains. Without the Way, Virtue would have no power. Without Virtue, the Way would have no appearance." (See his commentary to verse 21.) Han Fei put it more simply: "Te is the Tao at work." (See his commentary to verse 38.) Te is our entrance to the Tao. Te is what we cultivate. Lao-tzu's Virtue, however, isn't the virtue of adhering to a moral code but action that involves no moral code, no self, no other — no action.

These are the two poles around which the *Taoteching* turns: the Tao, the dark, the body, the essence, the Way; and Te, the light, the function, the spirit, Virtue. In terms of origin, the Tao comes first. In terms of practice, Te comes first. The dark gives the light a place to shine. The light allows us to see the dark. But too much light blinds. Lao-tzu saw people chasing the light and hastening their own destruction. He encouraged them to choose the dark instead of the light, less instead of more, weakness instead of strength, inaction instead of action. What could be simpler?

Lao-tzu's preference for darkness extended to himself as well. For the past 2,500 years, the Chinese have revered the *Taoteching* as they have no other text, and yet they know next to nothing about its author. What they do know, or think they know, is contained in a brief biographical sketch included by Ssu-ma Ch'ien in a history of ancient China he completed around 100 B.C. Although we don't know what Ssu-ma Ch'ien's sources were, we do know he was considered the most widely traveled man of his age, and he went to great lengths to verify the information he used. Of late it has become popular, if not *de rigueur*, to debunk his account of Lao-tzu. But it remains the earliest one we have and is worth repeating.

According to Ssu-ma Ch'ien, Lao-tzu was a native of Huhsien prefecture in the state of Ch'u. Nowadays, Huhsien is called Luyi. If you are traveling in China, or simply want to find it on a map, look for the town of Shangchiu/Shangqiu on the train line that runs between the city of Chengchou/Zhengzhou, the capital of Honan province, and the Grand Canal town of Hsuchou/Xuzhou to the east. Luyi is about seventy kilometers to the south of Shangchiu. The series of shrines that mark the site of Lao-tzu's former home is just east of town.

The region is known as the Huang-Huai Plain. As its name suggests, it is the result of the regular flooding of the Huangho, or Yellow River, to the north, and the Huaiho, or Huai River, to the south. The Chinese have been growing wheat and millet here since Neolithic times, and more recently cotton and tobacco. It remains one of the more productive agricultural areas of China, and it was a rich prize over which many ancient states fought.

Lao-tzu was born here in 604 B.C., or 571 B.C., depending on which account of later historians we accept. Ssu-ma Ch'ien doesn't give us a date. But he does say that Huhsien was part of the great state of Ch'u. Officially, Huhsien belonged to the small state of Ch'en until 479 B.C., when Ch'u eliminated Ch'en as a state once and for all. Some scholars have interpreted this to mean that either Huhsien did not belong to Ch'u when Lao-tzu was alive or that he must have been born there after 479 B.C. But we need not accept either conclusion. Ssu-ma Ch'ien would have been aware that Ch'u controlled the fortunes of Ch'en as early as 598 B.C., when Ch'u briefly annexed Ch'en then changed its mind and allowed Ch'en to exist as a "neighbor state."

Whether or not Huhsien was actually part of Ch'u is not important. What is important is that during the sixth century B.C., Ch'u controlled the region of which Huhsien was a part. This is significant not for verifying the accuracy of Ssu-ma Ch'ien's account but for directing our attention to the cultural influence that Ch'u represented.

Ch'u was not like the other states in the Central Plains. Although the rulers of Ch'u traced their ancestry to a grandson of the Yellow Emperor, the patriarch of

Chinese culture, they represented its shamanistic periphery. From their ancestral home in the Sungshan area, just south of the Yellow River, they moved, or were pushed, steadily southwest, eventually ending up in the Chingshan area, just north of the Yangtze. Over the centuries they mixed with other tribal groups, such as the Miao, and incorporated elements of their shamanistic cultures. The Ch'u rulers took for their surname the word *hsiung*, meaning "bear," and they called themselves Man or Yi, which the Chinese in the central states interpreted to mean "barbarians."

The influence of Ch'u's culture on Lao-tzu is impossible to determine, but it does help us better understand the *Taoteching*, knowing that it was written by a man who was no stranger to shamanistic conceptions of the sacred world. Certainly as Taoism developed in later centuries, it remained heavily indebted to shamanism, and some scholars even see evidence of the Ch'u dialect in the *Taoteching* itself.

This, then, was the region where Lao-tzu grew up. But his name was not Lao-tzu, which means "Old Master." Ssu-ma Ch'ien says his family name was Li, his personal name was Erh (meaning "ear," hence, learned), and his posthumous name was Tan (meaning "long-eared," hence, wise). In addition to providing us with a complete set of names, Ssu-ma Ch'ien also tells us that Lao-tzu, or Li Erh, served as keeper of the Chou dynasty's Royal Archives.

Before continuing, I should note that some scholars reject Ssu-ma Ch'ien's Li Erh or Li Tan and suggest instead a man named Lao Tan, who also served as keeper of the Royal Archives, but in the fourth century B.C. rather than the sixth. Some find this later date more acceptable in explaining Lao-tzu's innovative literary style as well as in explaining why Chuang-tzu (369–286 B.C.) attributes passages of the *Taoteching* to Lao Tan but not Li Tan. For his part, Ssu-ma Ch'ien was certainly familiar with Chuang-tzu's writings, and he was not unaware of the fourth-century historian Lao Tan. In fact, he admits that some people thought that Lao Tan was Lao-tzu. But Ssu-ma Ch'ien was not convinced that the two were the same man. After all, if Tan was Lao-tzu's posthumous name, why shouldn't Chuang-tzu and other later writers call him "Old Tan"? And why couldn't there be two record keepers with the same personal name in the course of two centuries? If China's Grand Historian was not convinced that the fourth-century historian was the author of the *Taoteching* — certainly he had more documents at his disposal than we now possess — I see no reason to decide in favor of a man whose only claim to fame was to prophesy the ascendancy of the state of Ch'in, which was to bring the Chou dynasty to an end in 221 B.C.

Meanwhile, back at the archives, I think I hear Lao-tzu laughing. The archives were kept at the Chou dynasty capital of Loyang. Loyang was a Neolithic campsite as early as 3000 B.C. and a military garrison during the first dynasties: the Hsia and the Shang. When the state of Chou overthrew the Shang in 1122 B.C., the Duke of Chou built a new, subsidiary capital around the old garrison. He dubbed it Wangcheng: City of the King. Usually, though, the Chou dynasty king lived in one of the new dynasty's two western capitals of Feng and Hao, both of which were just west of the modern city of Sian/Xian. But when these were destroyed in 771 B.C., Wangcheng became the sole royal residence. And this was where Lao-tzu spent his time recording the events at court.

And Lao-tzu must have been busy. When King Ching died in 520 B.C., two of his sons, Prince Chao and Prince Ching, declared themselves his successor. At first Prince Chao gained the upper hand, and Prince Ching was forced to leave the capital. But with the help of other nobles, Prince Ching soon returned and established another capital fifteen kilometers to the east of Wangcheng, which he dubbed Chengchou: Glory of Chou. And in 516 B.C., Prince Ching finally succeeded in driving his brother from the old capital.

In the same year, the keeper of the Royal Archives, which were still in Wangcheng, received a visitor from the state of Lu. The visitor was a young man named K'ung Fu-tzu, or Confucius. Confucius was interested in ritual and asked Lao-tzu about the ceremonies of the ancient kings.

According to Ssu-ma Ch'ien, Lao-tzu responded with this advice: "The ancients you admire have been in the ground a long time. Their bones have turned to dust. Only their words remain. Those among them who were wise rode in carriages when times were good and slipped quietly away when times were bad. I have heard that the clever merchant hides his wealth so his store looks empty and that the superior person acts dumb so he can avoid calling attention to himself. I advise you to get rid of your excessive pride and ambition. They won't do you any good. This is all I have to say to you." Afterward, Confucius told his disciples, "Today when I met Lao-tzu, it was like meeting a dragon."

The story of this meeting appears in a sufficient number of ancient texts to make it unlikely that it was invented by Taoists. Confucian records also report it taking place. According to the traditional account, Lao-tzu was eighty-eight years old when he met Confucius. If so, and if he was born in 604 B.C., the two sages would have met in 516 B.C., when Confucius would have been thirty-five. So it is possible.

Following his meeting with Confucius, Lao-tzu decided to take his own

HANKU PASS. Midway between the Chou dynasty's eastern and western capitals and situated between the Yellow River and the Chungnan Mountains. This is where Lao-tzu met Yin Hsi, Warden of the Pass. Photo by Bill Porter.

advice, and he left the capital by oxcart. And he had good reason to leave. For when Prince Chao was driven out of Wangcheng by his brother, he took with him the royal archives, the same archives of which Lao-tzu was in charge. If Lao-tzu needed a reason to leave, he certainly had one in 516 B.C.

With the loss of the archives, Lao-tzu was out of a job. He was also, no doubt, fed up with the prospects for enlightened rule in the Middle Kingdom. Hence, he headed not for his hometown of Huhsien, 300 kilometers to the east, but for the Hanku Pass, which was 150 kilometers west of Loyang, and which served as the border between the Chou dynasty's central states and the semibarbarian state of Ch'in, which controlled the area surrounding the dynasty's former western capitals.

As keeper of the Royal Archives, Lao-tzu no doubt supplied himself with the necessary documents to get through what was the most strategic pass in all of China. Hardly wide enough for two carts, it forms a seventeen-kilometer-long defile through a plateau of loess that has blown down from North China and accumulated between the Chungnan Mountains and the Yellow River over the past million years. In ancient times, the Chinese said that whoever controlled

Artist's depiction of Loukuantai on tiles. Photo by Bill Porter.

Hanku Pass controlled China. It was so easy to defend that during the Second World War the Japanese army failed to break through it, despite finding no difficulty in sweeping Chinese forces from the plains to the east.

Lao-tzu was expected. According to Taoist records, Master Yin Hsi was studying the heavens far to the west at the royal observatory of the state of Ch'in at a place called Loukuantai. One evening he noticed a purple vapor drifting from the east and deduced that a sage would soon be passing through the area. Since he knew that anyone traveling west would have to come through Hanku Pass, he proceeded to the pass.

Ssu-ma Ch'ien, however, says Yin Hsi was the Warden of the Pass and makes no mention of his association with Loukuantai. The connection with Loukuantai is based on later, Taoist records. In any case, when Lao-tzu appeared, Yin Hsi recognized the sage and asked for instruction. According to Ssu-ma Ch'ien, Lao-tzu then gave Yin Hsi the *Taoteching* and continued on to other, unknown realms.

Taoists, on the other hand, agree that Lao-tzu continued on from Hanku Pass, but in the company of Yin Hsi, who invited the sage to his observatory 250 kilometers to the west. Taoists also say Lao-tzu stopped long enough at Loukuantai to convey the teachings that make up his *Taoteching* and then traveled on through the Sankuan Pass, another 150 kilometers to the west, and into the state of Shu. Shu was founded by a branch of the same lineage that founded the state of Ch'u, although its rulers revered the cuckoo rather than the bear. And in the land of the cuckoo, Lao-tzu finally achieved anonymity as well as immortality.

Curiously, about six kilometers west of Loukuantai, there's a tombstone with Lao-tzu's name on it. The Red Guards knocked it down in the 1960s, and when I first visited Loukuantai, in 1989, it was still down. It has since been propped back up, and a small shrine built to protect it. On that first visit, I asked Loukuantai's abbot, Jen Fa-jung, what happened to Lao-tzu. Did he continue on through Sankuan Pass, or was he buried at Loukuantai? Master Jen suggested both stories were true. As Confucius noted, Lao-tzu was a dragon among men. And being a member of the serpent family, why should we wonder at his ability to leave his skin behind and continue on through cloud-barred passes?

And so Lao-tzu, whoever he was and whenever he lived, disappeared and left behind his small book. The book at first didn't have a title. When writers like Mo-tzu and Wen-tzu quoted from it in the fifth century B.C., or Chuang-tzu and Lieh-tzu in the fourth century B.C., or when Han Fei explained passages in the third century B.C. and Huai-nan-tzu in the second century B.C., they simply said, "Lao-tzu says this" or "Lao Tan says that." And so people started calling the source of all these quotes *Laotzu*.

Ssu-ma Ch'ien also mentioned no title. He said only that Lao-tzu wrote a book, and it was divided into two parts. About that same time, people started calling these two parts *The Way* and *Virtue*, after the first lines of verses 1 and 38. And to these were added the honorific *ching*, meaning "ancient text." And so Lao-tzu's book was called the *Tao-te-ching*, the *Book of Tao and Te*.

In addition to its two parts, it was also divided into separate verses. But, as with other ancient texts, the punctuation and enumeration of passages were left up to the reader. About the same time that Ssu-ma Ch'ien wrote his biography of Lao-tzu and people started calling the book the *Taoteching*, Yen Tsun produced a commentary in the first century B.C. that divided the text into seventy-two verses. A century earlier, or a couple of centuries later, no one knows which, Ho-shang Kung divided the same basic text into eighty-one verses. And a thousand years later, Wu Ch'eng tried a sixty-eight-verse division. But the system that has persisted through the centuries has been that of Ho-shang Kung.

The text itself has seen dozens of editions containing anywhere from five to six thousand characters. The numerical discrepancy is not as significant as it might seem, as it is largely the result of adding certain grammatical particles for clarity or omitting them for brevity. The greatest difference among editions centers not on the number of characters but on the rendering of certain phrases and the presence or absence of certain lines.

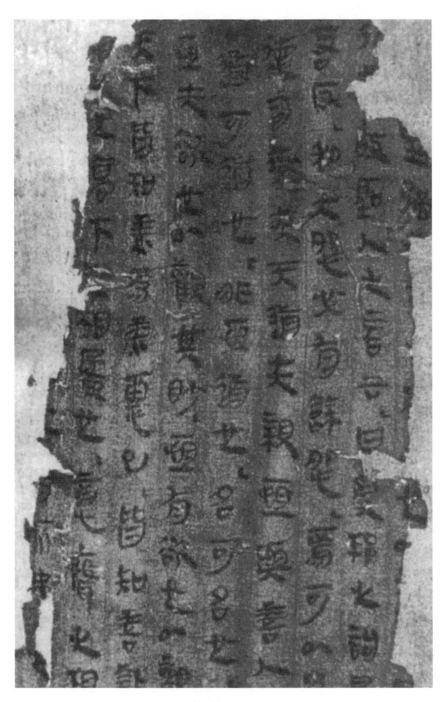

MAWANGTUI TEXT A. Written on silk shortly before 206 B.C., the text here shows verse 1 following verse 79, an arrangement unique to the Mawangtui texts. Photo by Steven R. Johnson.

Over the centuries, several emperors have even taken it upon themselves to resolve disputes concerning the choice among these variants. And the creation of standard editions resulted from their efforts. However, the standard editions were still open to revision, and every student seeking to understand the *Taoteching* repeats the process of choosing among variants.

In this regard, *Taoteching* studies were blessed in late 1973 with the discovery of two copies of the text in an ancient tomb. The tomb was located in the village of Mawangtui, a suburb of Changsha, the provincial capital of Hunan, and was sealed in 168 B.C. Despite the lapse of over 2,100 years, the copies, both written on silk, were in remarkably good condition.

Kao Chih-hsi, who supervised their removal and who directed the Mawangtui Museum for many years, attributes their preservation to layers of clay and charcoal that covered the tomb. At least this is his official explanation. In private, he says their preservation might have also been due to the presence of an unknown gas created by the decomposition of certain substances inside the tomb. He tried to take a sample of the gas, but the discovery was made in the middle of the Cultural Revolution, and he spent two days peddling his bicycle around Changsha before he found anyone who would loan him the necessary equipment. By then the gas was gone.

The books, though, made up for his disappointment. Along with the *Taoteching,* there were several hitherto unknown commentaries on the *Yiching* as well as a number of lost texts attributed to the Yellow Emperor. The Chinese Academy of Sciences immediately convened a committee of scholars to examine these texts and decipher illegible sections.

In the years since their discovery, the two Mawangtui copies of the *Taoteching* have contributed greatly to the elucidation of a number of difficult and previously misunderstood passages. Without them, I would have been forced to choose among unsatisfactory variants on too many occasions. Still, the Mawangtui texts contain numerous omissions and errors and need to be used with great care.

Fortunately, we have another text that dates from the same period. Like the Mawangtui texts, it was discovered in a tomb that was sealed shortly after 200 B.C. This tomb was located near the Grand Canal town of Hsuchou and was opened in A.D. 574. Not long afterward, the court astrologer, Fu Yi, published an edition of the copy of the *Taoteching* found inside.

In addition to the Mawangtui and Fuyi texts, we also have more than sixty copies that were found shortly after 1900 in the Silk Road oasis of Tunhuang. Most of these date from the eighth and ninth centuries. However, one of them was written by a man named Suo Tan in A.D. 270, giving us yet another early handwritten edition to consider.

We also have a copy of the *Taoteching* written by the great fourth-century calligrapher Wang Hsi-chih, as well as a dozen or so steles on which various emperors had the text carved. Finally, we have the text as it appears in such early commentaries as those of Yen Tsun, Ho-shang Kung, and Wang Pi, not to mention numerous passages quoted in the ancient works of Mo-tzu, Wen-tzu, Chuang-tzu, Lieh-tzu, Han Fei, Huai-nan-tzu, and others.

In undertaking this translation, I have consulted nearly all of these editions and have produced a new recension incorporating my choices among the different readings. For the benefit of those able to read Chinese, I have included the resulting text with my translation. I have also added a number of commentaries.

Over the centuries, some of China's greatest thinkers have devoted themselves to explaining the *Taoteching,* and no Chinese would consider reading the text without the help of at least one of these line-by-line or verse-by-verse explanations. When I first decided to translate the *Taoteching,* it occurred to me that Western readers are at a great disadvantage without the help of such materials. To remedy this, I have collected several dozen of the better-known commentaries, along with a few that are more obscure. And from these I have selected passages that provide important background information or insights.

Among the commentaries consulted, the majority of my selections come from a group of eleven men and one woman. In order of frequency of appearance, they include Su Ch'e, Ho-shang Kung, Wu Ch'eng, Wang Pi, Te-ch'ing, Sung Ch'ang-hsing, Li Hsi-chai, Lu Hui-ch'ing, Wang P'ang, Ch'eng Hsuan-ying, the Taoist nun Ts'ao Tao-ch'ung, and Wang An-shih. For the dates and a minimal amount of biographical information on these and other commentators, readers are directed to the glossary at the back of the book.

Readers will notice that I have restricted the comments to what could fit on facing pages. The reason for this is that I envisioned this book as a conversation between Lao-tzu and a group of people who have thought deeply about his text. And I wanted to have everyone, including the reader, in the same room, rather than in adjoining suites.

I have also added a few remarks of my own, though I have usually limited these to textual issues. In this regard, I have tried to restrict myself to those lines where my choice among variants may have resulted in a departure from other translations that readers might have in their possession. The *Taoteching* is, after all, one of the most translated books in the world, exceeded in this regard only by the Bible and the Bhagavad Gita.

The text was first translated into a Western language by the Jesuit missionary Joseph de Grammont, who rendered it into Latin shortly before 1788. Since then, more than a hundred translations have been published in Western languages alone (and no doubt hundreds more distributed privately among friends). Thus, readers could not be blamed for wondering if there isn't something inherent in the text that infects Westerners who know Chinese, and even those who don't, with the thought that the world needs yet another translation, especially one that gets it right.

My own attempt to add to this ever-growing number dates back nearly twenty-five years to when I attended a course in Taiwan given by John C.H. Wu. Professor Wu had himself produced an excellent English translation of the *Tao-teching*, and he offered a course on the subject to graduate students in the philosophy department of the College of Chinese Culture, which I was attending between stays at Buddhist monasteries.

Once a week, six of us filed past the guards at the stately Chungshanlou on Yangmingshan, where the government held its most important meetings and where Professor Wu lived in a bungalow provided to him in recognition of his long and distinguished service to the country. In addition to translating the *Tao-teching*, Professor Wu also translated the New Testament, drafted his country's constitution, and served as China's ambassador to the Vatican and its chief representative to the Hague.

One afternoon every week, we sipped tea, ate his wife's cookies, and discussed a verse or two of Lao-tzu's text. Between classes, I tried translating the odd line in the margins of Professor Wu's bilingual edition, but I did not get far. The course lasted only one semester, after which I moved to a Buddhist monastery in the hills south of Taipei and put aside Lao-tzu's text in favor of Buddhist sutras and poetry. But ever since then, I have been waiting for an opportunity to dust off this thinnest of ancient texts and resume my earlier attempt at translation.

The opportunity finally presented itself in 1993, when I returned to America after more than twenty years in Taiwan and Hong Kong. One day in the early seventies, when I was attending graduate school at Columbia University, Professor Bielenstein quoted W.A.C.H. Dobson, who said it was time for a Sinologist to retire when he announced he was working on a new translation of the *Taote-ching*. Having joined the ranks of those who spend their days at home, I figured I now qualified. Dobson's remarks, I suspect, were intended more as friendly criticism of the presumption that translating the *Taoteching* entails. Though relatively brief, it's a difficult text. But it's also a transparent one.

For the past two years, ever since I began working on my own presumptive addition to the world's *Taoteching* supply, one image that has repeatedly come to mind is skating on a newly frozen lake near my home in Idaho when I was a boy. Sometimes the ice was so clear, I felt like I was skating across the night sky. And the only sounds I could hear were the cracks that echoed through the dark, transparent depths. I thought if the ice ever gave way I would find myself on the other side of the universe. And I carried ice picks just in case I had to pull myself out. The ice never broke. But I've been hearing those cracks again.

Red Pine
First Quarter, Last Moon, Year of the Pig
Port Townsend, Washington

LAO-TZU'S TAOTECHING

1

玄之又玄。眾眇之門。
此兩者同。出而異名。
故恆無欲。以觀其眇。
無名天地之始。有名萬物之母。
恆有欲以觀其徼。
道可道。非恆道。名可名。非恆名。

The way that becomes a way

is not the Immortal Way

the name that becomes a name

is not the Immortal Name

no-name is the maiden of Heaven and Earth

name is the mother of all things

thus in innocence we see the beginning

in passion we see the end

two different names

for one and the same

the one we call dark

the dark beyond dark

the door to all beginnings

TU ER-WEI says, "*Tao* originally meant 'moon.' The *Yiching* [see hexagrams 42 and 52] stresses the bright moon, while Lao-tzu stresses the dark moon" (*Lao-tzu-te yueh-shen tsung-chiao*, pp. ii–iii).

CONFUCIUS says, "The Tao is what we can never leave. What we can leave isn't the Tao" (*Chungyung*: 1).

HO-SHANG KUNG says, "What we call a way is a moral or political code, while the Immortal Way takes care of the spirit without effort and brings peace to the world without struggle. It conceals its light and hides its tracks and can't be called a way. As for the Immortal Name, it's like a pearl inside an oyster, a piece of jade inside a rock: shiny on the inside, dull on the outside."

CH'ENG CHU says, "Sages don't reveal the Way because they keep it secret, but because it can't be revealed. Thus their words are like footsteps that leave no tracks."

LI HSI-CHAI says, "Things change but not the Tao. The Tao is immortal. It arrives without moving and comes without being called."

SU CH'E says, "The ways of kindness and justice change but not the way of the Tao.

No-name is its body. Name is its function. Sages embody the Tao and use it in the world. But while entering the myriad states of being, they remain in nonbeing."

WANG PI says, "From the infinitesimal all things develop. From nothing all things are born. When we are free of desire, we can see the infinitesimal where things begin. When we are subject to desire, we can see where things end. 'Two' refers to 'maiden' and 'mother.'"

TS'AO TAO-CH'UNG says, "'Two' refers to 'innocence' and 'passion,' or in other words, stillness and movement. Stillness corresponds to nonexistence. Movement corresponds to existence. Provisionally different, they are ultimately the same. Both meet in darkness."

THE SHUOWEN says, "Hsuan [dark] means 'black with a dot of red in it.'" This is how the darker half of the yin-yang symbol was traditionally represented. In Shensi province, where the Taoteching was first written, doors were, until recently, painted black with a thin line of red trim. And every road begins with a door.

TE-CH'ING says, "Lao-tzu's philosophy is all here. The remaining five thousand words only expand on this first verse."

During Lao-tzu's day, philosophers were concerned with the correspondence, or lack of it, between name and reality. The things we distinguish as real change, while their names do not. How then can reality be known through names? In lines two and four, I've used the Mawangtui heng (immortal) over the standard ch'ang (eternal), which was introduced to avoid an emperor's personal name. Heng also means "crescent moon," a not accidental usage in light of Lao-tzu's emphasis on lunar images when talking about the Tao. Around 1070 A.D. Ssu-ma Kuang and Wang An-shih punctuated lines five through eight in a way that made their subject wu (nonbeing) and yu (being). (Nonbeing is the name of the maiden of Heaven and Earth / being is the name of the mother of all things, and so on.) However, the grammatical particles in the Mawangtui texts make such a reading impossible. In line five, shih normally means "beginning." But China's earliest dictionary, the Shuowen, says, "Shih means 'a virgin.'" Ma Hsu-lun suggests shih in this case might also be a loan word for the nearly identical t'ai. While t'ai normally means "fetus," the Shuowen says it means "a woman in her third month of pregnancy." Note, too, that a woman did not receive her public name until after marriage. In lines seven and thirteen, most editions have miao (mysterious). But according to Pi Yuan, "In ancient times there was no miao [mysterious], only miao [small/beginning]," which is what we find in the Mawangtui texts. This verse is not present in the Kuotien texts.

3

2

天下皆知美。之為美。斯惡已。皆知善。之為善。斯不善已。有無相生。難易相成。長短相形。高下相盈。音聲相和。先後相隨。是以聖人處無為之事。行不言之教。萬物作焉而不嗣。為而不恃。功成而不居。夫唯不居。是以不去。

All the world knows beauty
but if that becomes beautiful
this becomes ugly
all the world knows good
but if that becomes good
this becomes bad
have and have not create each other
hard and easy produce each other
long and short shape each other
high and low complete each other
note and noise accompany each other
first and last follow each other
sages therefore perform effortless deeds
and teach wordless lessons
they don't look after all the things that arise
or depend on them as they develop
or claim them when they reach perfection
and because they don't claim them
they are never without them

LU HSI-SHENG says, "What we call beautiful or ugly depends on our feelings. Nothing is necessarily beautiful or ugly until feelings make it so. But while feelings differ, they all come from our nature, and we all have the same nature. Hence, sages transform their feelings and return to their nature and thus become one again."

WU CH'ENG says, "The existence of things, the difficulty of affairs, the size of forms, the magnitude of power, the pitch and clarity of sound, the sequence of position, all involve contrasting pairs. When one is present, both are present. When one is absent, both are absent."

LU HUI-CH'ING says, "These six pairs all depend on time and occasion. None of them is eternal. Sages, however, act according to the Immortal Tao. Hence, they act without effort. And because they teach according to the Immortal Name, they teach without words. Beautiful and ugly, good and bad don't enter their minds."

WANG WU-CHIU says, "Sages are not interested in deeds or words. They simply follow the natural pattern of things. Things rise, develop, and reach perfection. This is their order."

WANG AN-SHIH says, "Sages create but do not possess what they create. They act but do not depend on what they do. They succeed but do not claim success. These all result from selflessness. Because sages are selfless, they do not lose themselves. Because they do not lose themselves, they do not lose others."

SU CH'E says, "Losing something is the result of possessing something. How can people lose what they don't possess?"

LI HSI-CHAI says, "Lao-tzu's 5,000-word text clarifies what is mysterious as well as what is obvious. It can be used to attain the Tao, to order a country, or to cultivate the body."

HO-SHANG KUNG titles this verse: "Cultivating the Body."

SUNG CH'ANG-HSING says, "Those who practice the Way put an end to distinctions, get rid of name and form, and make of themselves a home for the Way and Virtue."

I have used the wording of the Mawangtui and Kuotien texts for lines seven through twelve but have omitted the Mawangtui insertion of *heng* (is endless) after line twelve. In line fifteen, I have followed the Kuotien wording: *ssu* (look after) in place of the usual *shih* (begin). Between lines fifteen and sixteen, neither the Mawangtui nor Kuotien copies include the line *sheng-er-pu-yu*, "or possess what they beget," which appears in the Wangpi and Fuyi editions and which was apparently interpolated from a similar sequence that appears in verse 51. The last two lines also appear in verse 77.

3

不上賢。使民不爭。不貴難得之貨
使民不為盜。不見可欲。使民不亂
是以聖人之治。虛其心。實其腹。
弱其志。強其骨。恆使民無知無欲
使夫知者不敢為。則無不治。

Bestowing no honors
keeps people from fighting
prizing no treasures
keeps people from stealing
displaying no attractions
keeps people from making trouble
thus the rule of the sage
empties the mind
but fills the stomach
weakens the will
but strengthens the bones
by keeping the people from knowing or wanting
and those who know from daring to act
the sage governs them all

SU CH'E says, "Bestowing honors embarrasses those who don't receive them to the point where they fight for them. Prizing treasures pains those who don't possess them to the point where they steal them. Displaying attractions distresses those who don't enjoy them to the point where they cause trouble. If people aren't shown these things, they won't know what to want and will cease wanting."

WANG CHEN says, "Sages empty the mind of reasoning and delusion, they fill the stomach with loyalty and honesty, they weaken the will with humility and compliance, and they strengthen the bones with what people already have within themselves."

WANG PI says, "Bones don't know how to make trouble. It's the will that creates disorder. When the mind is empty, the will is weak."

WANG P'ANG says, "An empty mind means no distinctions. A full stomach means no desires. A weak will means no external plans. Strong bones mean standing on one's own and remaining unmoved by outside forces. By bestowing no honors, sages keep people from knowing. Prizing no treasures, they keep people from wanting."

LU NUNG-SHIH says, "The mind knows and chooses, while the stomach doesn't know but simply contains. The will wants and moves, while bones don't want but simply stand there. Sages empty what knows and fill what doesn't know. They weaken what wants and strengthen what doesn't want."

YEN TSUN says, "They empty their mind and calm their breath. They concentrate their essence and strengthen their spirit."

HUANG YUAN-CHI says, "Sages purify their ears and eyes, put an end to dissipation and selfishness, embrace the one, and empty their mind. An empty mind forms the basis for transmuting cinnabar by enabling us to use our *yang* breath to transform our *yin* essence. A full stomach represents our final form, in which our *yang* breath gradually and completely replaces our *yin* essence."

WEI YUAN says, "The reason the world is in disorder is because of action. Action comes from desire. And desire comes from knowledge. Sages don't talk about things that can be known or display things that can be desired. This is how they bring order to the world."

LIU CHING says, "This verse describes how sages cultivate themselves in order to transform others."

Between the penultimate and final lines, the Fuyi edition and Tunhuang copy S.477 insert *wei-wu-wei,* "they act by not acting," while Mawangtui B has *wu-wei-er-yi,* "by simply not acting." Commentators who accept such versions often quote Confucius: "To govern without effort, that was Shun. And what did he do? He simply faced south and bowed" (*Lunyu*: 15.4). But such an emendation, however Taoist, is superfluous here, and was probably interpolated from elsewhere in the text. This verse is absent in the Kuotien texts.

4

道沖。而用之。又不盈。淵兮。
似萬物之宗。挫其銳。解其紛。
和其光。同其塵。湛兮。似或存。
吾不知其誰之子。象帝之先。

The Tao is so empty
those who use it
never become full again
and so deep
as if it were the ancestor of us all
it dulls our edges
unties our tangles
softens our light
and merges our dust
it's so clear
as if it were present
I wonder whose child it is
it seems it was here before Ti

WANG AN-SHIH says, "The Tao possesses form and function. Its form is the original breath that doesn't move. Its function is the empty breath that alternates between Heaven and Earth."

WU CH'ENG says, "'Empty' means 'empty like a bowl.' The Tao is essentially empty, and people who use it should be empty, too. To be full is contrary to the Tao. 'Deep' means 'what cannot be measured.' 'Ancestor' means 'one who unites a lineage,' just as the Tao unites all things. 'As if' suggests a reluctance to compare."

LI HSI-CHAI says, "The ancient masters of the Way had no ambition. Hence, they dulled their edges and did not insist on anything. They had no fear. Hence, they untied every tangle and avoided nothing. They did not care about beauty. Hence, they softened their light and forgot about themselves. They did not hate ugliness. Hence, they merged with the dust and did not abandon others."

WEI YUAN says, "By taking advantage of edges, we create conflicts with others. By shining bright lights, we illuminate their dust. Grinding down edges makes conflicts disappear. Dimming the light merges dust with dust and with darkness."

HUANG YUAN-CHI says, "A person who can adjust their light to that of the crowd and merge with the dust of the world is like a magic mushroom among ordinary plants. You can't see it, but it makes everything smell better."

HSI T'UNG says, "The Tao is invisible. Hence, Lao-tzu calls it 'clear.'"

THE SHUOWEN says, "Chan [clear] means 'unseen.'"

LU NUNG-SHIH says, "'Clear' describes what is deep, what seems to be present and yet not present, what seems to be not-present and yet not not-present."

LIU CHING says, "If it's empty, it's deep. If it's deep, it's clear. The Tao comes from nothing. Hence, the Tao is the child of nothing."

LI YUEH says, "Ti is the Lord of Creation. All of creation comes after Ti, except the Tao, which comes before it. But the nature of the Tao is to yield. Hence, Lao-tzu does not insist it came before. Thus, he says, 'it seems.'"

JEN CHI-YU says, "In ancient times no one denied the existence of Ti, and no one called his supremacy into doubt. Lao-tzu, however, says the Tao is 'the ancestor of us all,' which presumably included Ti as well" (Lao-tzu che-hsueh t'ao-lun-chi, p. 34).

For such an enigmatic verse, there are surprisingly few variants. In line three, I have gone along with the Fuyi edition, Tunhuang copy P.2584, and Mawangtui B in reading yu-pu-ying, "again not full," in place of huo-pu-ying, "seems not full." Because of problems resulting from their interpretation of the first four lines, some commentators think lines six through eight don't belong here. They do, in fact, also occur in verse 56, and could have been interpolated. However, I've read them as an explanation of the Tao's ancestral status, which makes kin of us all. This verse is absent in the Kuotien texts.

5

天地不仁。以萬物為芻狗。
聖人不仁。以百姓為芻狗。
天地之間。其猶橐籥乎。
虛而不屈。動而愈出。
多言數窮。不如守中。

Heaven and Earth are heartless
treating creatures like straw dogs
sages are heartless too
they treat people like straw dogs
between Heaven and Earth
how like a bellows
empty but inexhaustible
each stroke produces more
talking only wastes it
better to protect what's inside

HU SHIH says, "Lao-tzu's statement that Heaven and Earth are heartless undercuts the ancient belief that Heaven and Humankind were of the same lineage and thereby created the basis for natural philosophy" (*Chung-kuo-che-hsueh-shih ta-kang,* p. 56).

SU CH'E says, "Heaven and Earth aren't partial. They don't kill living things out of cruelty or give them birth out of kindness. We do the same when we make straw dogs to use in sacrifices. We dress them up and put them on the altar, but not because we love them. And when the ceremony is over, we throw them into the street, but not because we hate them. This is how sages treat the people."

HUAI-NAN-TZU says, "When we make straw dogs or clay dragons, we paint them yellow and blue, decorate them with brocade, and tie red ribbons around them. The shaman puts on his black robe, and the lord puts on his ceremonial hat to usher them in and to see them off. But once they've been used, they're nothing but clay and straw." A similar description appears in *Chuangtzu: 14.4.*

WU CH'ENG says, "Straw dogs were used in praying for rain, and these particular bellows were used in metallurgy."

WANG P'ANG says, "A bellows is empty so that it can respond. Something moves, and it responds. It responds but retains nothing. Like Heaven and Earth in regard to the ten thousand things or sages in regard to the people, it responds with what fits. It isn't tied to the present or attached to the past."

WANG AN-SHIH says, "The Tao has no substance or dimension, yet it works the breath of emptiness between Heaven and Earth and gives birth to the ten thousand things."

WANG TAO says, "The Tao cannot be talked about, yet we dismiss it as heartless. It cannot be named, yet we liken it to a bellows. Those who understand get the meaning and forget the words. Those who don't understand fail to see the truth and chatter away in vain."

HSIN TU-TZU says, "When the main path has many side trails, sheep lose their way. When learning leads in many directions, students waste their lives in study" (*Liehtzu: 8.25*).

HO-SHANG KUNG says, "Whenever the mouth opens and the tongue moves, disaster is close behind. Better to guard your inner virtue, nurture your vital essence, protect your spirit, treasure your breath, and avoid talking too much."

SUNG CH'ANG HSING says, "If our mouth doesn't talk too much, our spirit stays in our heart. If our ears don't hear too much, our essence stays in our genitals. In the course of time, essence becomes breath, breath becomes spirit, and spirit returns to emptiness."

Cultivating the heartless center between Heaven and Earth, sages delight in the endless creation of something out of nothing without becoming attached to anything. The Chinese phrase *pu-jen* (no heart) not only means "unkind" but also refers to any fruit that has no seed or kernel in its center. The straw dogs used in ceremonies in ancient China were much like Christmas trees in the West — used for a day, a week, a month, but not for long. The only textual variation of note involves the appearance in both Mawangtui texts of *wen* (hear) in place of *yen* (talk) in line nine. But since *wen* (hear) was often used for *wen* (ask), the meaning would not be significantly different whichever reading one prefers. I've retained the standard version. Lines five through eight are also present in the Kuotien texts.

6

谷神不死。是謂玄牝。玄牝之門。是謂天地之根。綿綿兮若存。用之不堇。

The valley spirit that doesn't die
we call the dark womb
the dark womb's mouth
we call the source of Heaven and Earth
as elusive as gossamer silk
and yet it can't be exhausted

THE *SHANHAICHING* says, "The Valley Spirit of the Morning Light is a black and yellow, eight-footed, eight-tailed, eight-headed animal with a human face" (9). The *Shanhaiching*'s "valley spirit" is the moon, which runs ahead of the sun during the last eight days of its thirty-day cycle, lags behind during the first eight days, and faces the sun during its eight days of glory. For the remaining days of the month, it's too close to the sun to be visible. Like many other cultures, the ancient Chinese viewed the moon as the embodiment of the female element of creation.

WANG PI says, "The valley is what is in the middle, what contains nothing, no form, no shadow, no obstruction. It occupies the lowest point, remains motionless, and does not decay. All things depend on it for their development, but no one sees its shape."

YEN FU says, "Because it is empty, we call it a 'valley.' Because there is no limit to its responsiveness, we call it a 'spirit.' Because it is inexhaustible, we say 'it doesn't die.' These three are the virtues of the Tao."

SU CH'E says, "A valley is empty but has form. A valley spirit is empty but has no form. What is empty and has no form is not alive. So how can it die? 'Valley spirit' refers to its virtue. 'Dark womb' refers to its capacity. This womb gives birth to the ten thousand things, and we call it 'dark' because we see it give birth but not how it gives birth."

HSUEH HUI says, "The words Lao-tzu chooses are often determined by the demands of rhyme and should not be restricted to their primary meaning. Thus, *p'in* [female animal] can also be read *p'in* [womb]."

HO-SHANG KUNG says, "The valley is what nourishes. Those able to nourish their spirit do not die. 'Spirit' means the spirits of the five organs: the gall bladder, the heart, the kidneys, and the spleen. When these five are injured, the five spirits leave. 'Dark' refers to Heaven. In a person, this means the nose, which links us with Heaven. 'Womb' refers to Earth. In a person, this means the mouth, which links us with Earth. The breath that passes through our nose and mouth should be finer than gossamer silk and barely noticeable, as if it weren't actually present. It should be relaxed and never strained or exhausted."

WU CH'ENG says, "The empty valley is where spirits dwell, where breath isn't exhausted. Who relaxes their breath increases their vitality. Who strains their breath soon expires."

TE-CH'ING says, "Purposeful action leads to exhaustion. The Tao is empty and acts without purpose. Hence, it can't be exhausted."

SUNG CH'ANG-HSING says, "The valley spirit, the dark womb, the source of Heaven and Earth all act without acting. That we don't see them doesn't mean they don't exist."

LIU CHING says, "It's like the silk of a silkworm or the web of a spider: hard to distinguish and hard to grab. But then, it isn't Humankind who uses it. Only the spirit can use it."

TU TAO-CHIEN says, "This verse also appears in *Liehtzu*: 1.1, where it is attributed to the Yellow Emperor instead of Lao-tzu. Lao-tzu frequently incorporates passages from ancient texts. We see their traces in 'thus the sage proclaims' or 'hence the ancients say.' Thus Confucius said, 'I don't create. I only relate' [*Lunyu*: 7.1]".

LIEH-TZU says, "What creates life is not itself alive" (*Liehtzu*: 1.1).

This is one of the few verses for which no significant textual variations exist. It is not present in the Kuotien texts.

7

故能成其私。
外其身。而身存。不以其無私邪。
是以聖人退其身。而身先。
以其不自生。故能長生。
天長地久。天地之所以能長且久者。

Heaven is eternal and Earth is immortal
the reason they're eternal and immortal
is because they don't live for themselves
hence they can live forever
sages therefore pull themselves back
and end up in front
put themselves outside
and end up safe
is it not because of their selflessness
whatever they seek they find

CHU CH'IEN-CHIH says, "The line 'Heaven is eternal and Earth is immortal' was apparently an old saying, which Lao-tzu quotes in order to explain its significance."

CHIANG SSU-CH'I says, "'Heaven' refers to the point between the eyebrows. 'Earth' refers to the point just below the navel."

LU HUI-CH'ING says, "Heaven stands for the movement of time. Earth represents the transformation of form. Heaven and Earth have their origin in the dark womb. And the essence of the dark womb is the valley spirit that doesn't die. Because it doesn't die, it isn't born. Only what isn't born can give birth to the living. And because it doesn't give birth to itself, it can live forever."

TS'AO TAO-CH'UNG says, "What is not alive is the basis for life. By equating life and death, we are no longer burdened by life and death. By abandoning bodily form, we are no longer hindered by bodily form."

WU CH'ENG says, "To pull oneself back means to be humble and not to try to be in front of others. To put oneself outside means to be content and not to try to add to one's life. To find what one seeks means to be in front and safe."

SUNG CH'ANG-HSING says, "Heaven and Earth help creatures fulfill their needs by not having any needs of their own. Can sages do otherwise? By following the Way of Heaven and Earth, sages are revered by all and harmed by none. Hence, they, too, live long."

JEN FA-JUNG says, "Sages do not purposely seek long life but achieve it through selflessness."

CH'ENG CHU says, "Heaven, Earth, and Humankind share the same origin. Why doesn't Humankind share their immortality? Because Heaven and Earth are not aware they are Heaven and Earth. Only Humankind is self-aware. And being self-aware, there is nothing humans won't do to stay alive. But the more they care for their life, the more pained their life becomes. The more they nourish their body, the sicker their body becomes. People who have not thought this out say the followers of Lao-tzu are afraid of death and only interested in immortality. But this is getting it backward."

HO-SHANG KUNG says, "The reason Heaven and Earth alone are eternal and immortal is because they are content and give without expecting a reward, unlike Humankind who never stops chasing profit and fighting over possessions."

WANG PI says, "Those who live for themselves fight with others. Those who don't live for themselves are the refuge of others."

SU CH'E says, "If Heaven and Earth fought with others over life, they would be the same as others. And if sages fought with others over profit, they would be the same as them. Would that not be a great shame?"

WANG P'ANG says, "Although sages are sages, they look the same as others. But because they embody the Way of Heaven and don't fight, they alone differ from everyone else. Sages are selfless because they no longer have a self."

LU TUNG-PIN says, "The only thing sages seek is Virtue."

Another verse with no major textual variations. It is also absent from the Kuo-tien texts.

8

上善若水。水善利萬物。而不爭。
處眾人之所惡。故幾於道。居善地。
心善淵。與善仁。言善信。政善治。
事善能。動善時。夫唯不爭。故無尤。

The best are like water
bringing help to all
without competing
choosing what others avoid
they thus approach the Tao
dwelling with earth
thinking with depth
helping with kindness
speaking with honesty
governing with peace
working with skill
and moving with time
and because they don't compete
they aren't maligned

WU CH'ENG says, "Among those who follow the Tao, the best are like water: content to be lower and, thus, free of blame. Most people hate being lower and compete to be higher. But when people compete, someone is maligned."

LI HUNG-FU says, "How do we know the best don't compete? Everyone else chooses nobility. They alone choose humility. Everyone else chooses the pure. They alone choose the base. What they choose is what everyone else hates. Who is going to compete with them?"

KUAN-TZU says, "Water is the source of creation, the ancestor of all living things. It's the bloodstream of Earth" (*Kuantzu*: 39).

HUANG YUAN-CHI says, "Mencius says, 'People cannot live without water and fire' [*Mencius*: 7A.23]. In terms of cultivation, when fire warms water, 'pure yang' arises. When water cools fire, 'sweet dew' appears."

WANG P'ANG says, "Water is the chief of the five elements [see verse 12]. It comes from space, which is not that far from the Tao."

WANG PI says, "The Tao does not exist, but water does. Hence, it only approaches the Tao."

HO-SHANG KUNG says, "The best people have a nature like that of water. They're like mist or dew in the sky, like a stream or a spring on land. Most people hate moist or muddy places, places where water alone dwells. The nature of water is like the Tao: empty, clear, and deep. As water empties, it gives life to others. It reflects without becoming impure, and there is nothing it cannot wash clean. Water can take any shape, and it is never out of touch with the seasons. How could anyone malign something with such qualities as this?"

SUNG CH'ANG-HSING says, "Those who free themselves from care stay low and avoid heights. Those whose minds are empty can plumb the depths. Those who help others without expecting any reward are truly kind. Those whose mouths agree with their minds speak the truth. Those who make demands of themselves as well as others establish peace. Those who can change as conditions change work with skill. Those who act when it is time to act and rest when it is time to rest move with time."

LI JUNG says, "Water has no purpose of its own. Those who can remain empty and not compete with others follow the natural Way."

YEN TSUN says, "If a ruler embodies this and uses this in his government, his virtue is most wonderful. How could he be maligned?"

HAN FEI says, "If a drowning man drinks it, he dies. If a thirsty man drinks it, he lives."

Given Lao-tzu's usual disdain for social virtues, some commentators have trouble accepting the standard reading of *jen* (kindness) in line eight. For those in search of an alternative, the Fuyi and Chinglung editions have *jen* (others), while Mawangtui B has *t'ien* (heaven), and Mawangtui A compresses lines eight and nine: "helping with honesty." This in not present in the Kuotien texts, yet it remains one of the *Taoteching*'s most quoted verses.

9

殖
而
盈
之
不
若
其
已
。

揣
而
銳
之
不
可
長
保
。

金
玉
盈
室
莫
之
能
守
。

富
貴
而
驕
自
遺
其
咎
。

功
遂
身
退
天
之
道
也
。

Instead of pouring in more
better stop while you can
making it sharper
won't help it last longer
rooms full of treasure
can never be safe
the vanity of success
invites its own failure
when your work is done retire
this is the Way of Heaven

THE *HOUHANSHU* says, "What Lao-tzu warns against is 'pouring in more'" (see the *Houhanshu*'s Lao-tzu biography).

HSUN-TZU says, "In the ancestral hall of Duke Huan, Confucius reports watching an attendant pour water into a container that hung at an angle. As the water level approached the midpoint, the container became upright. But when the attendant went beyond the midpoint, it tipped over, the water poured out, and only after it was empty did it resume its former position. Seeing this, Confucius sighed, 'Alas! Whatever becomes full becomes empty'" (*Hsuntzu*: 28).

LU TUNG-PIN says, "This verse is about the basics of cultivation. These are the obstacles when you first enter the gate."

LIU SHIH-LI says, "Since fullness always leads to emptiness, avoid satisfaction. Since sharpness always leads to dullness, avoid zeal. Since gold and jade always lead to worry, avoid greed. Since wealth and honor encourage excess, avoid pride. Since success and fame bring danger, know when to stop and where lies the mean. You don't have to live in the mountains and forests or cut yourself off from human affairs to enter the Way. Success and fame, wealth and honor are all encouragements to practice."

YEN TSUN says, "To succeed without being vain is easy to say but hard to practice. When success is combined with pride, it's like lighting a torch. The brighter it burns, the quicker it burns out."

WANG CHEN says, "To retire doesn't mean to abdicate your position. Rather, when your task is done, treat it as though it were nothing."

SSU-MA CH'IEN says, "When Confucius asked about the ceremonies of the ancients, Lao-tzu said, 'I have heard that the clever merchant hides his wealth so his store looks empty and that the superior man acts dumb to avoid calling attention to himself. I advise you to get rid of your excessive pride and ambition. They won't do you any good. This is all I have to say to you'" (*Shihchi*: 63).

HO-SHANG KUNG says, "Excessive wealth and desire wearies and harms the spirit. The rich should help the poor, and the powerful should aid the oppressed. If, instead, they flaunt their riches and power, they are sure to suffer disaster. Once the sun reaches the zenith, it descends. Once the moon becomes full, it wanes. Creatures flourish then wither. Joy turns to sorrow. When your work is done, if you do not step down, you will meet with harm. This is the Way of Heaven."

HUANG YUAN-CHI says, "You need a raft to cross a river. But once across, you can forget the raft. You need to study rules to learn how to do something. But once you know how, you can forget the rules."

This recipe for long life has been repeated in every civilized culture, and yet it has forever fallen on deaf ears. In the first line, the Kuotien texts have *chih* (amass) in place of the standard *ch'ih* (hold). Both Mawangtui texts have a similar character, also pronounced *chih*, which scholars consider to be a substitute for either *chih* (amass) or *ch'ih* (hold). I've sided with the Kuotien texts. Either way, the meaning amounts to the same thing. In line three, the Kuotien texts have *tuan-er-ch'un-chih*, "when floodwaters rise," which is clearly an anomaly, as it does not encourage a change in behavior but merely reflects a natural phenomenon.

10

載營魄抱一能無離。滌除玄鑒能如疵。專氣致柔能嬰兒。天門開闔能為雌。愛民治國能無為。生之畜之。明白四達能無知。生而不有。長而不宰。是謂玄德。

Can you keep your crescent soul from wandering
can you make your breath as soft as a baby's
can you wipe your dark mirror free of dust
can you serve and govern without effort
can you be the female at Heaven's Gate
can you light the world without knowledge
can you give birth and nurture
but give birth without possessing
raise without controlling
this is Dark Virtue

The Chinese say that the *hun,* or bright, ethereal, *yang* soul, governs the upper body and the *p'o,* or dark, earthly, *yin* soul, concerns itself with the lower body. Here, Lao-tzu mentions only the darker soul. But the word *p'o* also refers to the dark of the moon, and the opening phrase can also be read as referring to the first day of the new moon. Either way, dark of the soul or dark of the moon, Tao-ist commentators say the first line refers to the protection of our vital essence, of which semen and vaginal fluid, sweat and saliva are the most common examples, and the depletion of which injures the health and leads to early death.

HSUAN-TSUNG says, "The first transformation of life is called *p'o.* When the *p'o* becomes active and bright, it's called *hun.*"

WANG P'ANG says, "Life requires three things: vital essence, breath, and spirit."

CHIAO HUNG says, "The mind knows right and wrong. Breath makes no distinction. If we concentrate our breath and don't let the mind interfere with it, it remains soft and pure. Who else but a child can do this?"

CHUANG-TZU says, "The sage's mind is so still, it can mirror Heaven and Earth and reflect the ten thousand things" (*Chuangtzu:* 13.1).

WU CH'ENG says, "Our spirit dwells in our eyes. When the eyes see something, the spirit chases it. When we close our eyes and look within, everything is dark. But within the dark, we still see something. There is still dust. Only by putting an end to delusions can we get rid of the dust."

WANG AN-SHIH says, "The best way to serve is by not serving. The best way to govern is by not governing. Hence, Lao-tzu says, 'without effort.' Those who act without effort make use of the efforts of others. As for Heaven's Gate, this is the gate through which all creatures enter and leave. When it is open, it is active. When it is closed, it is still. Activity and stillness represent the male and the female. Just as stillness overcomes activity, the female overcomes the male." (The images of young women were often carved on either side of the entrance to ancient, subterranean tombs.)

SU CH'E says, "What lights up the world is the mind. There is nothing the mind does not know. And yet no one can know the mind. The mind is one. If someone knew it, there would be two. Going from one to two is the origin of all delusion."

LAO-TZU says, "The Way begets them / Virtue keeps them" (*Taoteching*: 51).

WANG PI says, "If we don't obstruct their source, things come into existence on their own. If we don't suppress their nature, things mature by themselves. Virtue is present, but its owner is unknown. It comes from the mysterious depths. Hence, we call it 'dark.'"

The first line has had numerous interpretations, to which I have added yet another. Most commentators agree that the character *tsai* should be placed at the beginning of this verse, instead of at the end of the previous verse, where it would function as equivalent to a punctuation mark indicating a rhetorical question. *Tsai* normally means "carry," but it can also mean "newly," as in the phrase *tsai-sheng-p'o*, "newly born dark moon/soul," or as Lao-tzu uses it here, *tsai-ying-p'o*, "newly lit dark moon/soul." In lines four and six, a number of editions invert "effort" and "knowledge." I have followed the edition of Ho-shang Kung and the arguments of Lo Chen-yu and Kao Heng in preferring the arrangement here. After line eight, most editions add *wei-er-pu-shih*, "develop without depending," which also appears in a similar sequence in verses 2 and 51 in some editions. I have followed the Mawangtui texts in omitting this line. This verse, which expresses Lao-tzu's yogic regimen more than any other in the *Taoteching*, is absent from the Kuotien texts.

11

卅輻共一轂。當其無。有車之用。埏埴以為器。當其無。有器之用。鑿戶牖以為室。當其無。有室之用。故有之以為利。無之以為用。

Thirty spokes converge on a hub
but it's the emptiness
that makes a wheel work
pots are fashioned from clay
but it's the hollow
that makes a pot work
windows and doors are carved for a house
but it's the spaces
that make a house work
existence makes a thing useful
but nonexistence makes it work

HSUAN-TSUNG says, "Thirty spokes converging on a hub demonstrates that less is the ancestor of more."

HO-SHANG KUNG says, "Ancient carts had thirty spokes in imitation of the lunar number."

LI JUNG says, "It's because the hub is empty that spokes converge on it. Likewise, it's because the minds of sages are empty that the people turn to them for help."

CH'ENG HSUAN-YING says, "A cart, a pot, and a house can hold things because they are empty. How much more those who empty their mind."

WU CH'ENG says, "All of these things are useful. But without an empty place for an axle, a cart can't move. Without a hollow place in the middle, a pot can't hold things. Without spaces for doors and windows, a room can't admit people or light. But these three examples are only metaphors. What keeps our body alive is the existence of breath within us. And it is our empty, nonexistent mind that produces breath."

SUNG CH'ANG-HSING says, "In this verse the Great Sage teaches us to understand the source by using what we find at hand. Doors refer to a person's mouth and nose. Windows refer to their ears and eyes."

CHANG TAO-LING says, "When ordinary people see these things, they only think about how they might employ them for their own advantage. When sages see them, they see in them the Tao and are careful in their use."

TE-CH'ING says, "Heaven and Earth have form, and everyone knows that Heaven and Earth are useful. But they don't know that their usefulness depends on the emptiness of the Great Way. Likewise, we all have form and think ourselves useful but remain unaware that our usefulness depends on our empty, shapeless mind. Thus, existence may have its uses, but real usefulness depends on nonexistence. Nonexistence, though, doesn't work by itself. It needs the help of existence."

HUANG YUAN-CHI says, "What is beyond form is the Tao. What has form are tools. Without tools we have no means to apprehend the Tao. And without the Tao there is no place for tools."

HSUEH HUI says, "At the end of this verse, Lao-tzu mentions both existence and nonexistence, but his intent is to use existence to show that nonexistence is more valuable. Everyone knows existence is useful, but no one pays attention to the usefulness of nonexistence."

Lao-tzu's "existence" and "nonexistence" are tantamount to *yang* and *yin*. There is no Kuotien text for this verse, and there are no significant textual variations, other than the omission in line seven of *yi-wei-shih*, "carved for a house," in both Mawangtui texts. Such an omission was, no doubt, a copyist error and suggests that neither text was actually used before it was placed in the tomb in which it was found, or it would have been corrected. Until recently, the people who lived in the middle reaches of the Yellow River watershed, where the *Taoteching* was composed, carved their houses out of the loess hillsides. As long as the ceilings of the rooms were carved in an arch, the compactness of the soil made support beams unnecessary. Thus, the only building materials needed were for doors and windows.

12

五色使人目盲。五音使人耳聾。馳騁田獵使人心發狂。

五味使人口爽。

難得之貨使人行妨。

是以聖人之治。為腹而不為目。

故去彼而取此。

The five colors make our eyes blind
the five tones make our ears deaf
the five flavors make our mouths numb
riding and hunting make our minds wild
hard-to-get goods make us commit crimes
thus the rule of the sages
favors the stomach over the eyes
thus they pick this over that

The early Chinese liked to divide everything into five basic states of existence. They distinguished things as made up of varying amounts of water, fire, wood, metal, and earth. And each of these came with its corresponding color: blue, red, black, white, and yellow; its corresponding flavor: salty, bitter, sour, pungent, and sweet; and its corresponding tone: la, sol, mi, re, and do.

YEN TSUN says, "Color is like an awl in the eye. Sound is like a stick in the ear. Flavor is like an ax through the tongue."

TE-CH'ING says, "When the eyes are given free rein in the realm of form, they no longer see what is real. When the ears are given free rein in the realm of sound, they no longer hear what is real. When the tongue is given free rein in the realm of flavor, it no longer tastes what is real. When the mind is given free rein in the realm of thought, it no longer knows what is real. When our actions are given free rein in the realm of possession and profit, we no longer do what is right. Like Chuang-tzu's tapir [*Chuangtzu*: 1.4], sages drink from the river, but only enough to fill their stomachs."

WU CH'ENG says, "Desiring external things harms our bodies. Sages nourish their breath by filling their stomach, not by chasing material objects to please their eyes. Hence, they choose internal reality over external illusion. But the eyes can't help seeing, and the ears can't help hearing, and the mouth can't help tasting, and the mind can't help thinking, and the body can't help acting. They can't stay still. But if we let them move without leaving stillness behind, nothing can harm us. Those who are buried by the dust of the senses or who crave sensory stimulation lose their way. And the main villain in this is the eyes. Thus, the first of Confucius' four warnings concerned vision [*Lunyu:* 12.1: not to look except with propriety], and the first of the Buddha's six sources of delusion was also the eyes."

LI YUEH says, "The eyes are never satisfied. The stomach knows when it is full."

SUNG CH'ANG-HSING says, "The main purpose of cultivation is to oppose the world of the senses. What the world loves, the Taoist hates. What the world wants, the Taoist rejects. Even though color, sound, material goods, wealth, and beauty might benefit a person's body, in the end they harm a person's mind. And once the mind wants, the body suffers. If we can ignore external temptations and be satisfied with the way we are, if we can cultivate our mind and not chase material things, this is the way of long life. All the treasures of the world are no match for this."

HSUAN-TSUNG says, "'Hard-to-get goods' refer to things that we don't possess by nature but that require effort to obtain. When we are not content with our lot and allow ourselves to be ruled by conceit, we turn our backs on Heaven and lose the Way."

CH'ENG HSUAN-YING says, "'That' refers to the blindness and delusion of the eyes. 'This' refers to the fullness and wisdom of the stomach."

I would add that "this" also refers to what is within easy reach, while "that" refers to what can be obtained only with effort. The Mawangtui texts present lines two through five in a different order: 4, 5, 3, 2. However, no other edition follows suit. Until as late as the early twentieth century, vast tracts of land in northern China were set aside for the exclusive use of the nobility and the military for conducting group hunts to practice their riding and archery. In line six, the standard editions do not include *chih-chih,* "the rule of." But it is present in both Mawangtui texts, and I have incorporated this variation in my translation. There is no Kuo-tien text for this verse.

13

寵辱若驚。貴大患若身。何謂寵辱若驚。

寵之為下。得之若驚。失之若驚。是謂寵辱若驚。

何謂貴大患若身。吾所以有大患者。為吾有身。

及吾無身。有何患。故貴以身於為天下。若可以寄天下。

若可以託天下。愛以身於為天下。若可以寄天下。

Favor and disgrace come with a warning
honor and disaster come with a body
why do favor and disgrace come with a warning
favor turns into disfavor
gaining it comes with a warning
losing it comes with a warning
thus do favor and disgrace come with a warning
and why do honor and disaster come with a body
the reason we have disaster
is because we have a body
if we didn't have a body
we wouldn't have disaster
thus those who honor their body more than the world
can be entrusted with the world
those who cherish their body more than the world
can be encharged with the world

WANG CHEN says, "People who are favored are honored. And because they are honored, they act proud. And because they act proud, they are hated. And because they are hated, they are disgraced. Hence, sages consider success as well as failure to be a warning."

SU CH'E says, "The ancient sages worried about favor as much as disgrace, because they knew that favor is followed by disgrace. Other people think favor means to ascend and disgrace means to descend. But favor cannot be separated from disgrace. Disgrace results from favor."

HO-SHANG KUNG says, "Those who gain favor or honor should worry about being too high, as if they were at the edge of a precipice. They should not flaunt their status or wealth. And those who lose favor and live in disgrace should worry more about disaster."

LU NUNG-SHIH says, "Why does favor become disgrace and honor become disaster? Favor and honor are external things. They don't belong to us. When we try to possess them, they turn into disgrace and disaster."

SSU-MA KUANG says, "Normally a body means disaster. But if we honor and cherish it and follow the natural order in our dealings with others, and we don't indulge our desires, we can avoid disaster."

HUANG YUAN-CHI says, "We all possess something good and noble that we don't have to seek outside ourselves, something that the glory of power or position cannot compare with. People need only start with this and cultivate this without letting up. The ancients said, 'Two or three years of hardship, ten thousand years of bliss.'"

WANG P'ANG says, "It isn't a matter of having no body but of guarding the source of life. Only those who refuse to trade themselves for something external are fit to receive the kingdom."

WANG PI says, "Those who are affected by favor and disgrace or honor and disaster are not fit to receive the kingdom."

TSENG-TZU says, "The superior person can be entrusted with an orphan or encharged with a state and be unmoved by a crisis" (*Lunyu: 8.6*).

The first two lines are clearly a quote, but commentators disagree about how to read them: are "favor" and "honor" verbs and "disgrace" and "disaster" their noun objects ("favor disgrace as a warning / honor disaster as your body")? Or are they both nouns, as I have read them? There is also the issue of how to read *juo*. Normally, it means "like" or "as." But it can also mean "to lead to," which is how Ho-shang Kung reads it, or "to entail" or "to come with," which is how I read it. An unusual usage, but it is after all a quote. Note, too, that in lines fourteen and sixteen, *juo* means "then," which I have left implied. In line three, the Kuotien texts, as well as some other editions (but not the Fuyi, Wangpi, or Mawangtui texts), omit *juo-ching*, "come with a warning." The last four lines are also found in *Chuangtzu: 11.2*, where they are used to praise the ruler whose self-cultivation doesn't leave him time to meddle in the lives of his subjects. They also appear in *Huainantzu: 12*, where they are used to praise the ruler who values the lives of his people more than the territory in which they live. In both cases, they agree with the Mawangtui version of lines thirteen and fifteen in reading *yu-wei-t'ien-hsia*, "more than the world," instead of the standard *wei-t'ien-hsia*, "as the world."

14

視之不見。名曰夷。聽之不聞。名曰希。搏之不得。名曰微。三者不可致詰。故絪而為一。其上不皦。其下不昧。繩繩兮不可名。復歸於無物。是謂無狀之狀。無物之象。是謂沕望。迎而不見其首。隨而不見其後。執今之道。以御今之有。以知古始。是謂道紀。

We look but don't see it

and call it indistinct

we listen but don't hear it

and call it faint

we reach but don't grasp it

and call it ethereal

three failed means to knowledge

I weave into one

with no light above

and no shadow below

too fine to be named

returning to nothing

this is the formless form

the immaterial image

the one that waxes and wanes

we meet without seeing its face

we follow without seeing its back

whoever upholds this very Way

can rule this very realm

and discover the ancient maiden

this is the thread of the Way

HO-SHANG KUNG entitles this verse "In Praise of the Dark" and says, "About what has no color, sound, or form, mouths can't speak and books can't teach. We can only discover it in stillness and search for it with our spirit. We cannot find it through investigation."

LU TUNG-PIN says, "We can only see it inside us, hear it inside us, and grasp it inside us. When our essence becomes one, we can see it. When our breath becomes one, we can hear it. When our spirit becomes one, we can grasp it."

CH'ENG HSUAN-YING says, "What we don't see is vital essence. What we don't hear is spirit. What we don't grasp is breath."

SU CH'E says, "People see things constantly changing and conclude something is there. They don't realize everything returns to nothing."

CH'EN KU-YING says, "'Nothing' doesn't mean nothing at all but simply no form or substance."

WANG PI says, "If we try to claim it doesn't exist, how do the myriad things come to be? And if we try to claim it exists, why don't we see its form? Hence, we call it 'the formless form.' But although it has neither shape nor form, neither sound nor echo, there is nothing it cannot penetrate and nowhere it cannot go."

LI YUEH says, "Everything is bright on top and dark on the bottom. But the Tao does not have a top or a bottom. Hence, it is neither bright nor dark. Likewise, we don't see its face because it never appears. And we don't see its back because it never leaves."

TS'AO TAO-CH'UNG says, "'This very realm' refers to our body."

LU HUI-CH'ING says, "The past isn't different from today, because we know what began in the past. And today isn't different from the past, because we know where today came from. What neither begins nor comes from anywhere else we call the thread that has no end. This is the thread of the Tao."

CHANG TAO-LING says, "The sages who achieved long life and immortality in the past all succeeded by means of this Tao. Whoever can follow their example today has found the thread of the Tao."

In line eight, I have anticipated the thread motif of lines eleven and twenty-one and have gone along with Mawangtui B in reading *chun* (weave) in place of the usual *hun* (merge). I have also preferred the Mawangtui versions of lines fifteen and eighteen, which the standard edition renders: "the one that is *indefinable*" and "upholding the *ancient* Way." The "face" and "back" we don't see refer to the darkness of the moon as it waxes and wanes. My reading of "ancient maiden" for *ku-shih* in line twenty, instead of the usual "ancient beginning," is based on an interpretation noted in verse one. This verse is absent in the Kuotien texts.

15

<table>
<tr><td>

保此道。不欲呈。夫唯不欲呈。是以能蔽而不成。

混兮其若濁。孰能濁。而靜之徐清。孰能安。以動之徐生。

嚴兮其若客。渙兮其若凌釋。敦兮其若朴。曠兮其若浴。

故強為之容。與兮其若冬涉川。猶兮其若畏四鄰。

古之善為士者。微眇。玄通。深不可識。夫唯不可識。

</td><td>

The great masters of ancient times
focused on the indiscernible
and penetrated the dark
you would never know them
and because you wouldn't know them
I describe them with reluctance
they were careful as if crossing a river in winter
cautious as if worried about neighbors
reserved like a guest
ephemeral like melting ice
simple like uncarved wood
open like a valley
and murky like a puddle
but those who can be like a puddle
become clear when they're still
and those who can be at rest
become alive when they're roused
those who treasure this Way
don't try to be seen
not trying to be seen
they can hide and stay hidden

</td></tr>
</table>

TS'AO TAO-CH'UNG says, "Although the ancient masters lived in the world, no one thought they were special."

SU CH'E says, "Darkness is what penetrates everything but what cannot itself be perceived. To be careful means to act only after taking precautions. To be cautious means to refrain from acting because of doubt or suspicion. Melting ice reminds us how the myriad things arise from delusion and never stay still. Uncarved wood reminds us to put an end to human fabrication and return to our original nature. A valley reminds us how encompassing emptiness is. And a puddle reminds us that we are no different from anything else."

HUANG YUAN-CHI says, "Lao-tzu expresses reluctance at describing those who succeed in cultivating the Tao because he knows the inner truth cannot be perceived, only the outward form. The essence of the Tao consists in nothing other than taking care. If people took care to let each thought be detached and each action well considered, where else would they find the Tao? Hence, those who mastered the Tao in the past were so careful they waited until a river froze before crossing. They were so cautious, they waited until the wind died down before venturing forth at night. They were orderly and respectful, as if they were guests arriving from a distant land. They were relaxed and detached, as if material forms didn't matter. They were as uncomplicated as uncarved wood and as hard to fathom as murky water. They stilled themselves to concentrate their spirit, and they roused themselves to strengthen their breath. In short, they guarded the center."

WANG PI says, "All of these similes are meant to describe without actually denoting. By means of intuitive understanding the dark becomes bright. By means of tranquillity, the murky becomes clear. By means of movement, the still becomes alive. This is the natural Way."

WANG CHEN says, "Those who treasure the Way fit in without making a show and stay forever hidden. Hence, they don't leave any tracks."

It would seem that Lao-tzu is also describing himself here. In line two, I have followed Mawangtui B in reading *miao* (aim/focus) for *miao* (mysterious). In lines fourteen and sixteen, I have followed the Kuotien, Wangpi, and Fuyi texts in adding *shu-neng* (who can) to the beginning of both lines. In line nineteen, I have followed the Kuotien texts, which have *ch'eng* (reveal) in place of the usual *ying* (full), and I have amended line twenty (again replacing *ying* with *ch'eng*) to fit this reading. Other variants of the last line include: "they can be old but not new" and "they can be old and again new." My reading is based on the Fuyi edition and Mawangtui B, as well as on the interpretations of Wang Pi and Ho-shang Kung, who also read *pi* (hide) instead of *pi* (old), thus recapitulating the opening lines as well as the two lines before it. The Kuotien texts omit lines five, twelve, and the last two lines.

16

致虛極。守靜督。萬物並作。吾以觀其復。夫物紜紜。各復歸其根。歸根曰靜。靜曰復命。復命曰常。知常曰明。不知常妄作凶。知常容。容乃公。公乃王。王乃天。天乃道。道乃久。沒身不殆。

Keeping emptiness as their limit
and stillness as their center
ten thousand things rise
we watch them return
creatures without number
return to their roots
returning to their roots they are still
being still they revive
reviving they endure
knowing how to endure is wisdom
not knowing is to suffer in vain
knowing how to endure is to yield
to yield is to be impartial
to be impartial is to be the ruler
the ruler is Heaven
Heaven is the Way
and the Way is long life
a life without trouble

SUNG CH'ANG-HSING says, "Emptiness is the Way of Heaven. Stillness is the Way of Earth. There is nothing that is not endowed with these. And everything rises by means of them."

LU HUI-CH'ING says, "What is meant here by emptiness is not utter emptiness but the absence of fullness. And what is meant by stillness is not complete stillness but everything unconsciously returning to its roots."

HUANG YUAN-CHI says, "Heaven has its fulcrum, people have their ancestors, and plants have their roots. And where are these roots? They are where things begin but have not yet begun, namely, the Dark Gate. If you want to cultivate the Great Way but don't know where this entrance is, your efforts will be in vain."

SU CH'E says, "We all rise from our nature and return to our nature, just as flowers and leaves rise from their roots and return to their roots, or just as waves rise from a river and return to the river. If you don't return to your nature, even if you still your actions and your thoughts, you won't be still. Heaven and Earth, mountains and rivers might be great, but none of them endures. Only what returns to its nature becomes still and enduring, while what does not return to its nature is at the mercy of others and cannot escape."

CH'ENG HSUAN-YING says, "Those who embrace all things and are impartial and selfless become great examples to others, who thus turn to them as their rulers."

TE-CH'ING says, "To know what truly endures is to know that Heaven and Earth share the same root, that the ten thousand things share one body, and that there is no difference between self and others. Those who cultivate this within themselves become sages, while those who practice this in the world become rulers. Rulers become rulers by following the Way of Heaven. And Heaven becomes Heaven by following the Tao. And the Tao becomes the Tao by lasting forever."

HO-SHANG KUNG says, "To know the unchanging course of the Way is to be free of passion and desire and to yield. To yield is to be free of self-interest. To be free of self-interest is to rule the world. To rule the world is to merge your virtue with that of Heaven. And to merge your virtue with that of Heaven is to be one with the Way. If you can do this, you will last as long as Heaven and Earth and live without trouble."

LI JUNG says, "Sages enjoy life without limits."

Our knowledge is the knowledge of twigs. Lao-tzu's knowledge is the knowledge of roots. In line two, the Kuotien, Wangpi, and Fuyi texts all have *tu* (substantial/true). But *tu* (substantial/true) was also used (especially with the "clothing" radical) as a variant of *tu* (the central seam at the back of a garment), which is what we find in Mawangtui B and which I have followed here. Mawangtui A has *piao* (show), but this was also used as another variant of *tu* (main seam). The Chinese character for "ruler" in lines fourteen and fifteen shows one vertically centered line connecting three horizontal lines: Heaven, Humankind, and Earth. The ruler was also called the Son of Heaven. Only the first six lines are present in the Kuotien texts.

17

太上下知有之。其次親譽之。
其次畏之。其次侮之。信不
足。安有不信。猶兮其貴言也。
成功遂事。而百姓謂我自然。

During the High Ages people knew they were there
then people loved and praised them
then they feared them
finally they despised them
when honesty fails
dishonesty prevails
hesitate and weigh your words
when their work succeeds
let people think they did it

The Chinese of Lao-tzu's day believed their greatest age of peace and harmony occurred during the reigns of the Three Sovereigns and Five Emperors, or 2,000 years earlier. These legendary rulers exercised power so unobtrusively, the people hardly knew they were there, as we hear in a song handed down from that distant age: "Sunup I rise / sundown I rest / I dig a well to drink / I plow fields to eat / the emperor's might / what is it to me?" (*Kushihyuan*: 1).

THE *LICHI* says, "During the High Ages people esteemed virtue. Then they worked for rewards" (1).

LU HSI-SHENG says, "The virtuous lords of ancient times initiated no actions and left no traces. Hence, the people knew they were there and that was all. When their virtue diminished, they ruled with kindness and justice, and the people loved and praised them. When their kindness and justice no longer controlled people's hearts, they governed with laws and punishments, and the people feared them. When their laws and punishments no longer controlled people's minds, they acted with force and deceit, and the people despised them."

MENCIUS says, "When the ruler views his ministers as his hands and feet, they regard him as their heart and soul. When he views them as dirt and weeds, they regard him as an enemy and a thief" (*Mencius*: 4B.3).

SUNG CH'ANG-HSING says, "The mistake of loving and praising, fearing and despising does not rest with the people but with those above. The reason the people turn to love and praise or fear and hate is because those above cannot be trusted. And when trust disappears, chaos appears."

HUANG YUAN-CHI says, "What we do to cultivate ourselves is what we do to govern the world. And among the arts we cultivate, the most subtle of all is honesty, which is the beginning and end of cultivation. When we embrace the truth, the world enjoys peace. When we turn our backs on the truth, the world suffers. From the time of the Three Sovereigns and Five Emperors, this has never varied."

HO-SHANG KUNG says, "When those above treat those below with dishonesty, those below respond with deceit."

WANG PI says, "Where there are words, there is a response. Thus, the sage hesitates."

WU CH'ENG says, "The reason sages don't speak or act is so they can bestow their blessings in secret and so people can live their lives in peace. And when their work succeeds and people's lives go well, people think that is just the way it is supposed to be. They don't realize it was made possible by those on high."

LU HUI-CH'ING says, "As long as the people think they did it themselves, they have no reason to love or praise anyone."

In line one, some editions have *pu-chih* (did not know) instead of *hsia-chih* (people [those below] knew), which is supported by the Mawangtui and Fuyi texts, as well as the Kuotien texts. The Fuyi text divides line two into two lines: "then they loved them / then they praised them." Despite the attractiveness of such a variation, placing *ch'in* (love) in a separate line interrupts the rhyme and is not supported by any other edition. The Kuotien texts begin the line that follows this verse with *ku* (therefore), and they are supported by both Mawangtui texts. Hence, it is likely that this verse was originally connected with the following verse, which it certainly is in terms of subject matter.

18

邦家昏亂。安有貞臣。
六親不和。安有孝慈。
智慧出。安有大偽。
大道廢。安有仁義。

When the Great Way disappears
we meet kindness and justice
when reason appears
we meet great deceit
when the six relations fail
we meet obedience and love
when the country is in chaos
we meet upright officials

Connecting this with the previous verse, WEI YUAN says, "What people love and praise are kindness and justice. What people fear is reason. And what people despise is deceit."

SUNG CH'ANG-HSING says, "It isn't the Great Way that leaves Humankind and goes into hiding. It's Humankind that leaves the Great Way and replaces it with kindness and justice."

SU CH'E says, "When the Great Way flourishes, kindness and justice are at work. But people don't realize it. Only after the Great Way disappears, do kindness and justice become visible."

WANG AN-SHIH says, "The Way hides in formlessness. Names arise from discontent. When the Way hides in formlessness, there isn't any difference between great or small. When names arise from discontent, we get distinctions such as kindness, justice, reason, and so forth."

HO-SHANG KUNG says, "When the kingdom enjoys peace, no one thinks about kindness, and the people are free of desire. When the Great Way prevails, kindness and justice vanish, just as the stars fade when the sun appears."

MENCIUS says, "Kindness means dwelling in peace. Justice means taking the right road" (*Mencius*: 4A.10).

TE-CH'ING says, "Reason is what the sage uses to order the kingdom. It includes the arts, measurements, and laws. In the High Ages, people were innocent, and these were unknown. In the Middle Ages, people began to indulge their feelings, and rulers responded with reason. And once reason appeared, the people responded with deceit."

WANG PI says, "The six relations are between father and son, elder and younger brothers, husband and wife. When these six relations are harmonious, the country governs itself, and there is no need for obedience, love, or honesty."

WANG P'ANG says, "During a virtuous age, obedience and love are considered normal. Hence, no one is called obedient or loving. Nowadays, when someone is obedient or loving, we praise them. This is because the six relations are no longer harmonious. Moreover, when peace prevails, everyone is honest. How can there be honest officials?"

CH'ENG HSUAN-YING says, "When the realm is at peace, loyalty and honesty are nowhere to be seen. Innocence and virtue appear when the realm is in chaos."

LI JUNG says, "During the time of the sage emperors Fu Hsi and Shen Nung, there was no mention of officials. It was only during the time of the despots Chieh and Chou that we begin to hear of ministers such as Kuan Lung-feng and Pi Kan."

WU CH'ENG says, "Shao Juo-yu assigns these four divisions to emperors, kings, the wise, and the talented."

Although I have left this verse in its traditional form, the Kuotien texts and both Mawangtui copies begin line one with *ku* (therefore), and some commentators have concluded that the two verses must have once been one. Lines three and four are missing in the Kuotien texts. Commentators often quote Chuang-tzu here: "When springs dry up, fish find themselves in puddles, spraying water on each other to keep each other alive. Better to be in a river or lake and oblivious of one another" (*Chuangtzu: 6.5*).

19

見素抱樸。少私寡欲。

此三言以為文未足。故令之有所屬。

民復孝慈。絕巧棄利。盜賊無有。

絕聖棄知。民利百倍。絕仁棄義。

Get rid of wisdom and reason
and people will live a hundred times better
get rid of kindness and justice
and people once more will love and obey
get rid of cleverness and profit
and thieves will cease to exist
but these three sayings are incomplete
hence let these be added
display the undyed and preserve the uncarved
reduce self-interest and limit desires

HO-SHANG KUNG says, "Get rid of the works of wisdom and reason and return to the primeval. The symbols and letters created by the Five Emperors were not as effective in ruling the kingdom as the simple knots used earlier by the Three Sovereigns."

TE-CH'ING says, "This is what Chuang-tzu meant when he said, 'Tigers and wolves are kind.' Tigers and wolves possess innate love and obedience that don't require instruction. How much more should Humankind, the most intelligent of creatures, possess these."

WANG CHEN says, "Put an end to wisdom that leaves tracks and reason that deceives, and people will benefit greatly. Put an end to condescending kindness and treacherous justice, and relatives will come together on their own and will once more love and obey. Put an end to excessive cleverness and personal profit, and armies will no longer appear. And when armies no longer appear, thieves will cease to exist."

HSUAN-TSUNG says, "These three only help us get rid of things. They don't explain cultivation. Hence, they are incomplete."

WANG PI says, "Wisdom and reason are the pinnacle of ability. Kindness and justice are the acme of behavior. Cleverness and profit are the height of practice. To tell us simply to get rid of them would be inappropriate and wouldn't make sense without giving us something else. Hence, we are told to focus on the undyed and the uncarved."

CHIAO HUNG says, "The ways of the world become daily more artificial. Hence, we have names like wisdom and reason, kindness and justice, cleverness and profit. Those who understand the Tao see how artificial these are and how inappropriate they are in ruling the world. They aren't as good as getting people to focus their attention on undyed cloth and uncarved wood. By displaying what is undyed and preserving what is uncarved, our self-interest and desires wane. The undyed and the uncarved refer to our original nature."

LIU CHING says, "'Undyed' means unstained by anything else and thus free of wisdom and reason. 'Uncarved' means complete in itself and thus free of kindness and justice. 'Self-interest' concerns oneself. And 'desires' concern others. As they diminish, so do cleverness and profit."

SU CH'E says, "Confucius relied on kindness and justice, ritual and music to order the kingdom. Lao-tzu's only concern was to open people's minds, which he accomplished through the use of metaphor. Some people, though, have used his metaphors to create disorder, while no great problems have been caused by the followers of Confucius."

Get rid of sayings, and people will be their own sages. The Kuotien texts invert lines five and six with lines three and four. They also have a puzzling character in line seven in place of *wen* (sayings). Some scholars think the character in question is a variant of *pian* (distinctions), while others think it's a variant of *shih* (directives). In either case, it isn't supported by any other edition. However, the Kuotien texts have been helpful in adding their weight to the Wangpi and Fuyi editions, which place the line, "Get rid of learning and problems will vanish," at the beginning of the next verse rather than at the end of this one, which is what I have also done.

20

絕學無憂。唯與訶。其相去幾何。美與惡。其相去何若。人之所畏。
亦不可不畏。望兮其未央哉。眾人熙熙。若饗於大牢。而春登臺。我泊焉未兆。
若嬰兒未咳。累兮若無所歸。眾人皆有餘。我獨若遺。我愚人之心也。純純兮。
俗人昭昭。我獨若昏兮。俗人察察。我獨湣湣兮。沕兮其若海。望兮其若無所止。
眾人皆有以。我獨頑且鄙。我獨欲異於人。而貴食母。

Get rid of learning and problems will vanish
yes and no
aren't so far apart
lovely and ugly
aren't so unalike
what others fear
we can't help fear too
before the moon begins to wane
everyone is overjoyed
as if they were at the Great Sacrifice
or climbing a tower in spring
I sit here and make no sign
like an infant that doesn't smile
lost with no one to turn to
while others enjoy more
I alone seem deficient
with a mind like that of a fool
I'm so simple
others look bright
I alone seem dim
others are certain
I alone am confused
ebbing like the ocean
waxing without cease
everyone has a goal
I alone am dumb and backward
for I alone choose to differ
preferring still my mother's tit

CH'ENG HSUAN-YING says, "When we give up the study of phenomena and understand the principle of noninterference, troubles come to an end and distress disappears."

LI HSI-CHAI says, "What passes for learning in the world never ends. For every truth found, two are lost. And while what we find brings joy, losses bring sorrow — sorrow that never ends."

CH'ENG HSUAN-YING says, "*Wei* [yes] indicates agreement and *k'o* [no] disdain."

SUNG CH'ANG-HSING says, "Even though 'yes' and 'no' come from the same source, namely the mouth, 'yes' is the root of beauty, and 'no' is the root of ugliness. Before they appear, there is nothing beautiful or ugly and nothing to fear. But once they appear, if we don't fear one or the other, disaster and harm are unavoidable."

LI HSI-CHAI says, "What others love, the sage also loves. What others fear, the sage fears, too. But where the sage differs is that while others don't see anything outside their own minds, the mind of the sage wanders in the Tao."

WANG P'ANG says, "Everything changes into its opposite. Beginning follows end without cease. But people think everything is either beautiful or ugly. How absurd! Only the sage knows that the ten thousand ages are the same, that nothing is gained or lost."

SU CH'E says, "People all drown in what they love: the beauty of the Great Sacrifice, the happiness of climbing to a scenic viewpoint in spring. Only the sage sees into their illusory nature and remains unmoved. People chase things and forget about the Tao, while the sage clings to the Tao and ignores everything else, just as an infant only nurses at its mother's breast."

TS'AO TAO-CH'UNG says, "People all seek external things, while sages alone nourish themselves on internal breath. Breath is the mother, and spirit is the child. The harmony of mother and child is the key to nourishing life."

Another verse in which Lao-tzu chooses the crescent moon, while others choose the full moon. In ancient China, emperors marked the return of swallows to their capitals in spring with the Great Sacrifice to the Supreme Intermediary, while people of all ranks climbed towers or hiked into the hills to view the countryside in bloom and to celebrate the first full moon. In line eight, I have followed Mawangtui B in reading *wang* (full [or waxing] moon) instead of the usual *huang* (boundless). I have used the same variant in line twenty-four. The Kuotien texts have only the first seven lines of this verse.

21

孔德之容。唯道是從。道之為物。唯恍唯惚。惚兮恍兮。中有象兮。恍兮惚兮。中有物兮。窈兮冥兮。中有精兮。其精甚真。其中有信。自今及古。其名不去。以順眾父。吾何以知眾父之然也。以此。

The appearance of Empty Virtue
this is what comes from the Tao
the Tao as a thing
waxes and wanes
it waxes and wanes
but inside is an image
it wanes and waxes
but inside is a creature
it's distant and dark
but inside is an essence
an essence that is real
inside which is a heart
throughout the ages
its name hasn't changed
so we might follow our fathers
how do we know what our fathers were like
by means of this

WANG PI says, "Only when we take emptiness as our virtue can our actions accord with the Tao."

SUNG CH'ANG-HSING says, "Sages have it. So does everyone else. But because others are selfish and attached, their virtue isn't empty."

HUANG YUAN-CHI says, "Emptiness and the Tao are indivisible. Those who seek the Tao cannot find it except through emptiness. But formless emptiness is of no use to those who cultivate the Tao."

YEN LING-FENG says, "Virtue is the manifestation of the Way. The Way is what Virtue contains. Without the Way, Virtue would have no power. Without Virtue, the Way would have no appearance."

SU CH'E says, "The Tao has no form. Only when it changes into Virtue does it have an appearance. Hence, Virtue is the Tao's visual aspect. The Tao neither exists nor does not exist. Hence, we say it waxes and wanes, while it remains in the dark unseen."

CH'ENG HSUAN-YING says, "The true Tao exists and yet does not exist. It does not exist and yet does not not exist. Lao-tzu says it waxes and wanes to stress that the Tao is not separate from things, and things are not separate from the Tao. Outside of the Tao, there are no things. And outside of things, there is no Tao."

WU CH'ENG says, "'Inside' refers to Virtue. 'Image' refers to the breath of something before it is born. 'Creature' refers to the form of something after it is born. 'Distant and dark' refers to the utter invisibility of the Tao."

CHANG TAO-LING says, "Essence is like water: the body is its embankment, and Virtue is its source. If the heart is not virtuous, or if there is no embankment, water disappears. The immortals of the past treasured their essence and lived, while people today lose their essence and die."

WANG P'ANG says, "Essence is where life and the body come from. Lao-tzu calls it 'real' because once things become subject to human fabrication, they lose their reality."

LIU CHING says, "Everything changes, and names are no exception. What was true in the past is false today. Only the Tao is constant."

In China people trace their descent through their male parent. The male is visible, the female hidden. Lao-tzu is nourished by his mother (Tao) but follows his father (Te). The Mawangtui texts have introduced a number of variants into this verse. Those I have incorporated into my translation include *wang* (full [and hence waxing] moon) for *huang* (indistinct) in lines four, five, and seven; *shun* (follow) for *yueh* (view) in line fifteen; and *fu* (father) for *fu* (beginning) in lines fifteen and sixteen. The use of "father" here was, I suggest, intended to balance the appearance of "mother" in the previous verse. The standard version of lines fifteen and sixteen reads: "so we might view our beginnings / and how do we know what our beginnings were like." Also, in line twelve, I have read *hsin* (lamp wick), and hence "the heart of something," in place of the word's usual meaning as "talisman," and hence something trustworthy. This verse is not present in the Kuotien texts.

22

曲則全。枉則直。窪則盈。敝則新。少則得。
多則惑。是以聖人執一。以為天下牧。不自視故章。
不自見故明。不自伐故有功。不自矜故能長。
夫唯不爭。故莫能與之爭。古之所謂曲則全者。
幾語哉。成全歸之。

The incomplete become whole
the crooked become straight
the hollow become full
the worn-out become new
those with less become content
those with more become confused
sages therefore hold on to one thing
and use this to guide the world
not considering themselves they appear
not displaying themselves they shine
not flattering themselves they succeed
not parading themselves they lead
because they don't compete
no one can compete against them
the ancients who said the incomplete become whole
came close indeed
becoming whole depends on this

CHUANG-TZU says, "Lao-tzu said everyone else seeks happiness. He alone saw that to be incomplete was to become whole" (*Chuangtzu: 33.5*).

WU CH'ENG says, "By exploring one side to its limits, we eventually find all sides. By grasping one thing, we eventually encompass the whole. The caterpillar bends in order to straighten itself. A hollow in the ground fills with water. The renewal of spring depends on the withering of fall. By having less, it's easy to have more. By having more, it's easy to become confused."

WANG PI says, "As with a tree, the more of it there is, the farther it is from its roots. The less of it there is, the closer it is to its roots. 'More' means more distant from what is real. 'Less' means closer."

WEI YUAN says, "One is the extreme of less. But whoever uses this as the measure for the world always finds more."

LU HUI-CH'ING says, "Only those who find but one thing can act like this. Thus to have less means to be content. The reason most people cannot act like this is because they have not found one thing. Thus, to have too much means to be confused."

LI HSI-CHAI says, "The reason sages are able to be chief of all creatures is because they hold on to one thing. Holding on to this one thing, they never leave the Tao. Hence, they do not observe themselves but rely instead on the vision of others. They do not talk about their own strengths but rely instead on the strengths of others. They stand apart and do not compete. Hence, no one can compete against them."

HSUAN-TSUNG says, "Not observing themselves, they become whole. Not displaying themselves, they become upright. Not flattering themselves, they become complete. Not parading themselves, they become new."

TZU-SSU says, "Only those who are perfectly honest can realize their nature and help others do the same. Next are those who are incomplete" (*Chungyung*: 22–23).

MENCIUS says, "We praise those who don't calculate. We reproach those who try to be whole" (*Mencius*: 4A.21).

HO-SHANG KUNG says, "Those who are able to practice being incomplete keep their physical body whole. Those who depend on their mother and father suffer no harm."

Lao-tzu's path to wholeness is through incompleteness, but an incompleteness so incomplete that he is reduced to one thing. For the wording of lines eight through thirteen, as well as line sixteen, I have followed Mawangtui B. Lines nine through twelve appear in slightly different form in verse 24. In the last line, my use of *ch'eng* (become), in place of the usual *ch'eng* (honest), is based on Tunhuang texts S.6453 and P.2584, as well as on the Suichou and Chinglung editions, and also on Chu Ch'ien-chih's observation that *ch'eng* (honest) appears nowhere else in the *Taoteching*, while *ch'eng* (become) occurs seventeen times. The interpolation of "honest" was apparently influenced by the passage from Tzu-ssu's *Chungyung* quoted above. Note that the images in the first six lines are also used to refer to the moon.

23

希言自然。飄風不終朝。暴雨不終日。孰為此。天地。天地而不能久。況於人乎。故從事。而道者同於道。得者同於得。失者同於失。同於得者。道亦得之。同於失者。道亦失之。

Whispered words are natural
a gale doesn't last all morning
a squall doesn't last all day
who creates these
Heaven and Earth
if Heaven and Earth can't make things last
how much less can Humankind
thus in whatever you do
when you follow the Way be one with the Way
when you succeed be one with success
when you fail be one with failure
be one with success
for the Way succeeds too
be one with failure
for the Way fails too

WU CH'ENG says, "'Whispered' means not heard. 'Whispered words' mean no words. Those who reach the Tao forget about words and follow whatever is natural."

WANG CHEN says, "Whispered words require less effort. Hence, they conform to the natural Way."

LU NUNG-SHIH says, "Something is natural when nothing can make it so, and nothing can make it not so."

CH'ENG HSUAN-YING says, "If the greatest forces wrought by Heaven and Earth cannot last, how can the works of Humankind?"

SU CH'E says, "The words of sages are faint, and their deeds are plain. But they are always natural. Hence, they can last and not be exhausted."

TE-CH'ING says, "This verse explains how sages forget about words, embody the Tao, and change with the seasons. Elsewhere, Lao-tzu says, 'Talking only wastes it / better to conserve the inside' [verse 5]. Those who love to argue get farther from the Way. They aren't natural. Only those whose words are whispered are natural. Lao-tzu uses wind and rainstorms as metaphors for the outbursts of those who love to argue. They can't maintain such a disturbance and dissipation of breath very long. Because they don't really believe in the Tao, their actions don't accord with the Tao. They haven't learned the secret of how to be one."

CHIAO HUNG says, "Those who pursue the Way are natural. Natural means free from success and hence free from failure. Such people don't succeed and don't fail but simply go along with the successes and failures of the age. Or if they do succeed or fail, their minds are not affected."

LU HUI-CH'ING says, "Those who pursue the Way are able to leave their selves behind. No self is the Way. Success. Failure. I don't see how they differ."

HO-SHANG KUNG says, "Those who are one with success enjoy succeeding. Those who are one with failure enjoy failing. Water is wet, and fire burns. This is their nature."

Success, failure, both lead to the Way. But the path of failure is shorter. Many commentators have found the latter half of the standard version of this verse confusing and marked by an awkward use of rhythm and rhyme. I have used the simpler and smoother Mawangtui version. However, in lines ten, twelve, and thirteen, I have followed the Fuyi text's use of *te* (succeed) in place of *te* (virtue). Both characters were interchangeable when the *Taoteching* was composed, but using "virtue" here leaves one with the problem as to how one can lose virtue and still be one with the Way. The Wangpi and Fuyi versions add this couplet to the end of the verse: "Where honesty fails / dishonesty prevails." But these lines appear to have been interpolated from verse 17 and are not present in either Mawangtui text. Nor do they follow from the rest of this verse, in rhyme or in meaning. This verse is not present in the Kuotien texts.

24

物其自自跂
或在伐視者
惡道者者不
之日無不立
。。功章。
故餘。。跨
有食自自者
道贅矜見不
者行者者行
不。不不。
處　長明
。　。。

Those who tiptoe don't stand
those who stride don't walk
those who consider themselves don't appear
those who display themselves don't shine
those who flatter themselves achieve nothing
those who parade themselves don't lead
travelers have a saying
too much food and a tiring pace
some things are simply bad
those who possess the Way thus shun them

TE-CH'ING says, "People raise themselves up on their tiptoes to see over the heads of others, but they cannot stand like this for long. People take longer strides to stay in front of others, but they cannot walk like this very far. Neither of these is natural."

WU CH'ENG says, "To tiptoe is to lift the heels in order to increase one's height. To stride is to extend the feet in order to increase one's pace. A person can do this for a while but not for long. Likewise, those who consider themselves don't appear for long. Those who display themselves don't shine for long. Those who flatter themselves don't succeed for long. And those who parade themselves don't lead for long."

SU CH'E says, "Anyone can stand or walk. But if those who are not content with standing tiptoe to extend their height or those who are not content with walking stride to increase their speed, their stance and their pace are sure to suffer. It's the same with those who consider themselves, or display themselves, or flatter themselves, or parade themselves. It's like eating or drinking. As soon as you're full, stop. Overeating will make you ill. Or it's like manual work. As soon as you're done, quit. Overwork will only exhaust you."

SUNG CH'ANG-HSING says, "Selfless and free of desire is the mind of the sage. Conniving and clever is the mind of the common person. Observing themselves, displaying themselves, flattering themselves, and parading themselves, they hasten their end, like someone who eats too much."

LI HSI-CHAI says, "Those who cultivate the Tao yet still think about themselves are like people who overeat or overwork. Food should satisfy the hunger. Work should suit the task. Those who keep to the Way do only what is natural."

LU HUI-CH'ING says, "Why should Taoists avoid things? Doesn't the Tao dwell in what others avoid? [see verse 8.] Taoists don't avoid what others hate, namely humility and weakness. They only avoid what others fight over, namely flattery and ostentation. Hence, they avoid some things and not others. But they never fight."

CHANG TAO-LING says, "Who follows the Way lives long. Who loses the Way dies early. This is the unbiased law of Heaven. It doesn't depend on offerings or prayers."

Line two does not appear in either Mawangtui text but does appear in all other texts and is needed here to establish the rhyme. In line two, *k'ua* (stride) can also mean "straddle." Ts'ao Tao-ch'ung says, "Those who straddle two sides are unsure of the Way." Lines three through six also appear in slightly different form in verse 22, and some commentators have read 22 and 24 as a single verse. For the wording and order of lines three through six, I have followed the Mawangtui texts, which reverse lines three and four and which have *shih* (consider/observe) in place of the standard *shih* (approve). A number of commentators think line eight is corrupt and suggest instead: "leftover food and a cyst-covered body." Although sufficiently repulsive, this is not the sort of warning we would expect of seasoned travelers of the Way. The last two lines also appear as lines two and three in verse 31. This verse is absent in the Kuotien texts.

25

人法地。地法天。天法道。道法自然。

遠曰反。道大。天大。地大。王亦大。國中有四大。而王居一焉。

吾不知其名。字之曰道。吾強為之。名曰大。大曰逝。逝曰遠。

有物混成。先天地生。蕭兮寥兮。獨立而不垀。可以為天下母。

Imagine a nebulous thing
here before Heaven and Earth
subtle and elusive
dwelling apart and unconstrained
it could be the mother of us all
not knowing its name
I call it the Tao
forced to describe it
I describe it as great
great means ever-flowing
ever-flowing means far-reaching
far-reaching means returning
the Tao is great
Heaven is great
Earth is great
the ruler is also great
the realm contains Four Greats
of which the ruler is but one
Humankind imitates Earth
Earth imitates Heaven
Heaven imitates the Tao
and the Tao imitates itself

WU CH'ENG says, "'Nebulous' means complete and indivisible."

SU CH'E says, "The Tao is neither pure nor muddy, high nor low, past nor future, good nor bad. Its body is a nebulous whole. In Humankind it becomes our nature. It doesn't know it exists, and yet it endures forever. And within it are created Heaven and Earth."

LI HSI-CHAI says, "It dwells apart but does not dwell apart. It goes everywhere but does not go anywhere. It's the mother of the world, but it's not the mother of the world."

SUNG CH'ANG-HSING says, "The Tao does not have a name of its own. We force names upon it. But we cannot find anything real in them. We would do better returning to the root from which we all began."

Standing beside a stream, CONFUCIUS sighed, "To be ever-flowing like this, not stopping day or night!" (*Lunyu:* 9.16).

TS'AO TAO-CH'UNG says, "Although we say it's far-reaching, it never gets far from itself. Hence, we say it's returning."

HO-SHANG KUNG says, "The Tao is great because there is nothing it does not encompass. Heaven is great because there is nothing it does not cover. Earth is great because there is nothing it does not support. And the king is great because there is nothing he does not govern. Humankind should imitate Earth and be peaceful and pliant, plant and harvest its grains, dig and discover its springs, work without exhaustion and succeed without fuss. As for Earth imitating Heaven, Heaven is still and immutable. It gives without seeking a reward. It nourishes all creatures and takes nothing for itself. As for Heaven imitating the Tao, the Tao is silent and does not speak. It directs breath and essence unseen, and thus all things come to be. As for the Tao imitating itself, the nature of the Tao is to be itself. It does not imitate anything else."

WANG PI says, "If Humankind does not turn its back on Earth, it brings peace to all. Hence it imitates Earth. If Earth does not turn its back on Heaven, it supports all. Hence, it imitates Heaven. If Heaven does not turn its back on the Tao, it covers all. Hence, it imitates the Tao. And if the Tao does not turn its back on itself, it realizes its nature. Hence, it imitates itself."

At the end of line four, I've followed the Kuotien and Mawangtui texts (and also *Huainantzu:* 2) in reading *kai* (border/restriction) in place of *kai* (change), which is what appears in the Wangpi and Fuyi editions. I've also followed the Kuotien texts and both Mawangtui texts in not including the line that follows line four in the Wangpi and Fuyi editions: *chou-hsing-er-pu-tai*, "travels everywhere without moving." The first five lines once again recall the image of the moon. The character for "ruler" (*wang:* 王) shows three horizontal lines (Heaven, Humankind, Earth) connected by a single vertical line. Lao-tzu's point is that the ruler, being only one of the four great powers of the world, should not be so presumptuous of his greatness, for he depends on the other three.

26

輕則失本。躁則失君。

如何萬乘之主。而以身輕於天下。

雖有環官。燕處超然。

是以君子終日行。不離其輜重。

重為輕根。靜為躁君。

Heavy is the root of light
still is the master of restless
thus a lord might travel all day
but never far from his supplies
even in a guarded camp
his manner is calm and aloof
why would the lord of ten thousand chariots
treat himself lighter than his kingdom
too light he loses his base
too restless he loses command

HAN FEI says, "'Heavy' means to be in control of oneself. 'Still' means not to leave one's place. Those who are heavy control those who are light. Those who are still direct those who are restless."

WANG PI says, "Something light cannot support something heavy. Something small cannot hold down something large."

CONFUCIUS says, "A gentleman without weight is not held in awe, and his learning is not secure" (*Lunyu*: 1.8).

CH'ENG HSUAN-YING says, "Roots are heavy, while flowers and leaves are light. The light wither, while the heavy survive. 'Still' means tranquil, and 'restless' means excited. Excitement is subject to birth and death. Tranquillity endures. Hence, the still rule the restless."

TE-CH'ING says, "'Heavy' refers to the body. 'Light' refers to what is external to the body: success and fame, wealth and honor. 'Still' refers to our nature. 'Restless' refers to our emotions. People forget their body and chase external things. They forget their nature and follow their emotions. Sages aren't like this. Even though they travel all day, they don't leave what sustains them."

KUAN-TZU says, "Those who move lose their place. Those who stay still are content" (quoted by Chiao Hung).

WU CH'ENG says, "When a lord travels for pleasure, he rides in a passenger carriage. When a lord travels to battle, he rides in a war chariot. Both of these are light. And behind these come the heavier baggage carts. Even though a lord might travel fifty kilometers a day in a passenger carriage or thirty kilometers a day in a war chariot, he does not hurry so far ahead that he loses sight of the baggage carts behind him."

TS'AO TAO-CH'UNG says, "'Supplies' means the precious commodities with which we maintain ourselves and without which we cannot exist for a second."

HO-SHANG KUNG says, "A lord who is not heavy is not respected. A plant's leaves and flowers are light. Hence, they are blown about by the wind. And its roots are heavy. Hence, it lives long. A lord who is not still loses his power. A dragon is still. Hence, it is able to constantly transform itself. A tiger is restless. Hence it dies young."

HSUAN-TSUNG says, "Traditionally, the Son of Heaven's fief included one million neighborhoods with a tax revenue of 640,000 ounces of silver, one million cavalry horses, and ten thousand war chariots. Hence, he was called 'lord of ten thousand chariots.'"

SU CH'E says, "If the ruler is light, his ministers know he cannot be relied upon. If the ministers are restless, the ruler knows their minds are bent on profit."

A number of commentators have wondered if the standard *jung-kuan* (glorious scenes) in line five might not be a mistake for *ying-kuan* (military camp). The Mawangtui texts have borne them out, though with *huan-kuan* (guarded camp). Line eight, which the Mawangtui texts clarify by adding *yu* (than), recalls the last four lines of verse 13. In line nine, I have gone along with the Mawangtui and Fuyi texts as well as with several early commentaries and editions in reading *pen* (base) in place of *ch'en* (minister). This verse is not present in the Kuotien texts.

27

善行者無徹迹。善言者無瑕讁。善數者不以籌筭。
善閉無關籥。而不可啟。善結無繩約。而不可解。
是以聖人恆善救人。故無棄人。物無棄財。
是謂襲明。故善人不善人之師。
不貴其師。不愛其資。唯知大眯。此謂眇眇。

Good walking leaves no tracks
good talking contains no flaws
good counting counts no beads
good closing locks no locks
and yet it can't be opened
good tying ties no knots
and yet it can't be undone
sages are good at saving others
therefore they abandon no one
nor anything of use
this is called cloaking the light
thus the good instruct the bad
and the bad learn from the good
not honoring their teachers
or cherishing their students
the wise alone are perfectly blind
this is called peering into the distance

LU TUNG-PIN says, "'Good' refers to our original nature before our parents were born. Before anything develops within us, we possess this goodness. 'Good' means natural."

HO-SHANG KUNG says, "Those who are good at walking find the Way within themselves, not somewhere outside. When they talk, they choose their words. When they count, they don't go beyond one. When they close, they close themselves to desire and protect their spirit. When they tie, they secure their mind."

TE-CH'ING says, "Sages move through the world with an empty self and accept the way things are. Hence, they leave no tracks. They do not insist that their own ideas are right and accept the words of others. Hence, they reveal no flaws. They do not care about life and death, much less profit and loss. Hence, they count no beads. They do not set traps, yet nothing escapes them. Hence, they use no locks. They are not kind, yet everyone flocks to them. Hence, they tie no knots."

WANG PI says, "These five tell us to refrain from acting and to govern things by relying on their nature rather than on their form."

WU CH'ENG says, "The salvation of sages does not involve salvation, for if someone is saved, someone is abandoned. Hence, sages do not save anyone at all. And because they do not save anyone, they do not abandon anyone. To 'cloak' means to use an outer garment to cover an inner garment. If the work of salvation becomes apparent, and people see it, it cannot be called good. Only when it is hidden is it good."

CH'ENG HSUAN-YING says, "The good always cloak their light."

HSUAN-TSUNG says, "The good are like water. Free of impurity and without effort on their part, they show people their true likeness. Thus, they instruct the bad. But unless students can forget the teacher, their vision will be obscured."

SU CH'E says, "Sages do not care about teaching. Hence, they do not love their students. And the world does not care about learning. Hence, people do not honor their teachers. Sages not only forget the world, they make the world forget them."

Lao-tzu apparently took his own advice regarding teachers and students, all of whom remain nameless. I have used the Mawangtui version of line ten, which replaces two lines in the standard editions: "they are good at saving things / thus they abandon nothing." For the last two characters of the last line, I have followed the word order of the Fuyi and Wangpi editions. However, I have chosen the Mawangtui *miao* (peer) in place of the standard *miao* (mystery), and I have read the standard *yao* (essential) as shorthand for *yao* (distant). This verse is not present among the Kuotien texts.

28

知其雄。守其雌。為天下奚。為天下奚。恆德不離。復歸於嬰兒。知其白。守其辱。為天下谷。為天下谷。恆德乃足。復歸於樸。知其白。守其黑。為天下式。為天下式。恆德不忒。恆德不忒。復歸於無極。樸散則為器。聖人用之則為官長。夫大制無割。

Recognize the male
but hold on to the female
and be the world's maid
being the world's maid
don't lose your Immortal Virtue
not losing your Immortal Virtue
be a newborn child again
recognize the pure
but hold on to the base
and be the world's valley
being the world's valley
be filled with Immortal Virtue
being filled with Immortal Virtue
be a block of wood again
recognize the white
but hold on to the black
and be the world's guide
being the world's guide
don't stray from your Immortal Virtue
not straying from your Immortal Virtue
be without limits again
a block of wood can be split to make tools
sages make it their chief official
a master tailor doesn't cut

TE-CH'ING says, "To recognize the Way is hard. Once you recognize it, holding on to it is even harder. But only by holding on to it can you advance on the Way."

MENCIUS says, "The great person does not lose their child heart" (*Mencius*: 4B.12).

WANG TAO says, "Sages recognize 'that' but hold on to 'this.' 'Male' and 'female' mean hard and soft. 'Pure' and 'base' mean noble and humble. 'White' and 'black' mean light and dark. Although hard, noble, and light certainly have their uses, hard does not come from hard but from soft, noble does not come from noble but from humble, and light does not come from light but from dark. Hard, noble, and light are the secondary forms and farther from the Way. Soft, humble, and dark are the primary forms and closer to the Way. Hence, sages return to the original: a block of wood. A block of wood can be made into tools, but tools cannot be made into a block of wood. Sages are like blocks of wood, not tools. They are the chief officials and not functionaries."

CH'ENG HSUAN-YING says, "What has no limits is the Tao."

CONFUCIUS says, "A great person is not a tool" (*Lunyu*: 2.12).

CHANG TAO-LING says, "To make tools is to lose sight of the Way."

SUNG CH'ANG-HSING says, "Before a block of wood is split, it can take any shape. But once split, it cannot be round if it is square or straight if it is curved. Lao-tzu tells us to avoid being split. Once we are split, we can never return to our original state."

PAO-TING says, "When I began butchering, I used my eyes. Now I use my spirit instead and follow the natural lines" (*Chuangtzu*: 3.2).

WANG P'ANG says, "Those who use the Tao to tailor leave no seams."

In lines three and four, I have followed Tunhuang copies P.2584 and S.6453 in reading *hsi* (maid/female servant) for the standard *hsi* (stream) as more in keeping with the images of the preceding lines. In lines eight through twenty-one, I have followed the Mawangtui texts, which fail to support the suspicions of some commentators that these lines were interpolated. Reverence for the spirit of wood is still shared by many of the ethnic groups along China's borders. During Lao-tzu's day, the southern part of his own state of Ch'u was populated by the Miao, who trace their ancestry to a butterfly and the butterfly to the heart of a maple tree. It has been suggested that Lao-tzu was somehow affiliated with the Miao, if not through blood or family ancestry then marriage. This verse is not present in the Kuotien texts. Instead of the usual *ch'ang* (immortal/constant), I have preferred the character *heng* (immortal/constant), present in both Mawangtui texts, as it also means "crescent moon" and is used by Lao-tzu elsewhere in the *Taoteching* with both the lunar image and immortality in mind, as in verse 1. The last four lines recall the images and wording of the first two lines in verse 16.

29

將欲取天下而為之。吾見其不得已。夫天下神器也。非可為者也。為者敗之。執者失之。夫物或行。或隨。或呴。或吹。或培。或墮。是以聖人去甚。去奢。去泰。

Trying to govern the world with force
I see this not succeeding
the world is a spiritual thing
it can't be forced
to force it is to harm it
to control it is to lose it
sometimes things lead
sometimes they follow
sometimes they blow hot
sometimes they blow cold
sometimes they expand
sometimes they collapse
sages therefore avoid extremes
avoid extravagance
avoid excess

SUNG CH'ANG-HSING says, "We can't control something as insignificant as a mustard seed. How can we control something as big as the world?"

TE-CH'ING says, "Those who would govern the world should trust what is natural. The world cannot be controlled consciously. It is too big a thing. The world can only be governed by the spirit, not by human strength or intelligence."

HO-SHANG KUNG says, "Spiritual things respond to stillness. They cannot be controlled with force."

LU HUI-CH'ING says, "The world as a thing is a spiritual thing. Only the spiritual Tao can control a spiritual thing. Spiritual things don't think or act. Trying to control them with force is not the Way."

WANG CHEN says, "'Force' refers to the mobilization and deployment of troops. But the world's spirit cannot be controlled with weapons."

LI HSI-CHAI says, "Sages consider their body as transitory and the world as its temporary lodging. How can they rule what is not theirs and lose the true and everlasting Way?"

SU CH'E says, "The interchange of *yin* and *yang*, of high and low, of great and small is the way things are and cannot be avoided. Fools are selfish. They insist on having their own way and meet with disaster. Sages know they cannot oppose things. They agree with whatever they meet. They eliminate extremes and thereby keep the world from harm."

WU CH'ENG says, "How do those who gain control of the world keep the world from harm? Sages understand that things necessarily move between opposites but that there is a way to adjust this movement. Things that prosper too much must wither and die. By keeping things from prospering too much, they keep them from withering and dying."

WANG PI says, "Sages penetrate the nature and condition of others. Hence, they respond to them without force and follow them without effort. They eliminate whatever misleads or confuses others so that their minds become clear and each realizes their own nature."

WANG AN-SHIH says, "Resting where you are eliminates extremes. Treasuring simplicity eliminates extravagance. Being content with less eliminates excess."

LU NUNG-SHIH says, "Sages get rid of extremes with kindness. They get rid of extravagance with simplicity. They get rid of excess with humility. By means of these three, sages govern the world."

HSUEH HUI says, "What Lao-tzu means by 'extremes,' by 'extravagance,' and by 'excess' is not what people mean nowadays. Lao-tzu means whatever involves an increase in effort beyond what is easy."

Lao-tzu's word for the world is *tien-hsia* (under Heaven) — all that we see when we look down from on high. For the wording of lines nine and ten, I have followed Ho-shang Kung. Between lines ten and eleven, most editions add a fourth pair of opposites: *ch'iang-lei* (strengthen-weaken). I have followed Mawangtui B, which has only three pairs. Given the three negations at the end of this verse, three pairs to be negated seems more appropriate. This verse is not present in the Kuotien texts.

30

物壯則老。是謂不道。不道早已。
果而勿伐。果而不得已矣。是謂果而不強。
不以取強焉。果而勿驕。
師之所居。楚棘生之。善者果而已矣。
以道佐人主。不以兵強於天下。其事好還。

Use the Tao to assist your lord
don't use weapons to rule the land
such things have repercussions
where armies camp
brambles grow
best to win then stop
don't make use of force
win but don't be proud
win but don't be vain
win but don't be cruel
win when you have no choice
this is to win without force
virility leads to old age
this isn't the Tao
what isn't the Tao ends early

SUNG CH'ANG-HSING says, "A kingdom's ruler is like a person's heart: when the ruler acts properly, the kingdom is at peace. When the heart works properly, the body is healthy. What enables them to work and act properly is the Tao. Hence, use nothing but the Tao to assist a ruler."

LI HSI-CHAI, quoting *Mencius* (7B.7), says, "'If you kill someone's father, someone will kill your father. If you kill someone's brother, someone will kill your brother.' This is how things have repercussions."

CH'ENG HSUAN-YING says, "The external use of soldiers and arms returns in the form of vengeful enemies. The internal use of poisonous thoughts come back in the form of evil rebirths."

WANG AN-SHIH says, "Humankind's retribution is clear, while Heaven's retribution is obscure. Where an army spends the night, brambles soon appear. In an army's wake, bad years follow. This is the retribution of Heaven."

WANG CHEN, paraphrasing *Suntzu Pingfa* (2.1), says, "To raise an army of a hundred thousand requires the daily expenditure of a thousand ounces of gold. And an army of a hundred thousand means a million refugees on the road. Also, nothing results in greater droughts, plagues, or famines than the scourge of warfare. A good general wins only when he has no choice, then stops. He dares not take anything by force."

MENCIUS says, "Those who say they are great tacticians or great warriors are, in fact, great criminals" (*Mencius*: 7B.2–3).

LU HUI-CH'ING says, "To win means to defeat one's enemies. To win without being arrogant about one's power, to win without being boastful about one's ability, to win without being cruel about one's achievement, this sort of victory only comes from being forced and not from the exercise of force."

SU CH'E says, "Those who possess the Tao prosper and yet seem poor. They become full and yet seem empty. What is not virile does not become old and does not die. The virile die. This is the way things are. Using an army to control the world represents the height of strength. But it only hastens old age and death."

HO-SHANG KUNG says, "Once plants reach their height of development, they wither. Once people reach their peak, they grow old. Force does not prevail for long. It isn't the Tao. What is withered and old cannot follow the Tao. And what cannot follow the Tao soon dies."

WU CH'ENG says, "Those who possess the Way are like children. They come of age without growing old."

LAO-TZU says, "Tyrants never choose their death" (*Taoteching*: 42).

It isn't the Tao that ends early, for the Tao has no beginning or end. I have not followed the Kuotien texts in omitting lines four and five, or lines eleven, thirteen, fourteen, and fifteen, or in placing line three at the end of this verse. However, I have gone along with the Kuotien and also the Mawangtui texts in omitting lines six and seven of the standard edition: "in an army's wake / bad years follow." I have also followed the Mawangtui sequence of lines eight through ten. The last three lines also appear in verse 55. Since these lines aren't present in the Kuotien texts, some commentators have suggested that they might have been interpolated here as a commentary. However, they are present in both Mawangtui texts and all standard editions. Hence, I've retained them.

31

夫唯兵者不祥之器也。物或惡之。故有道者不處。君子居則貴左。

用兵則貴右。兵者不祥之器也。故兵者非君子之器也。不得已而用之。

恬惔為上。故不美也。若美之。是樂殺人。夫樂殺人。

不可以得志於天下矣。是以吉事上左。喪事上右。是以偏將軍處左。

上將軍處右。言以喪禮處之也。殺人眾。以悲哀泣之。戰勝。而以喪禮處之。

Weapons are not auspicious tools
some things are simply bad
thus the Taoist shuns them
in peace the ruler honors the left
in war he honors the right
weapons are not auspicious tools
he wields them when he has no choice
dispassion is the best
thus he doesn't praise them
those who praise their use
enjoy killing others
those who enjoy killing others
achieve no worldly rule
thus we honor the left for happiness
we honor the right for sorrow
the left is where the adjutant stands
the commander on the right
which means as at a funeral
when you kill another
honor him with your tears
when the battle is won
treat it as a wake

HO-SHANG KUNG says, "In times of decadence and disorder, we use weapons to defend the people."

SU CH'E says, "We take up weapons to rescue the distressed and not as a matter of course."

SUNG CH'ANG-HSING says, "The system of ritual devised by the ancient kings treated the right as superior and the left as inferior. Being superior, the right represented the Way of Victory. Being inferior, the left represented the Way of Humility. But victory entails death and destruction. Hence, those on the right were in charge of sad occasions, while those on the left were in charge of happy events."

JEN FA-JUNG says, "'Left' refers to the east and the power of creation, while 'right' refers to the west and the power of destruction."

HSUAN-TSUNG says, "When Tibetans, Huns, or other tribes invade our borders, the ruler has no choice but to respond. But he responds as he would to a gnat. He does not act in anger. The greatest victory involves no fighting. Hence, dispassion is the best policy."

LI HSI-CHAI says, "Sun-tzu discussed in detail the use of strengths and weaknesses and of direction and indirection in warfare. But he did not understand their basis (*Suntzu Pingfa*: 5–6). Lao-tzu says dispassion is the best policy, because it secures victory without a display. This might seem odd, but dispassion means to rest, and rest is the root of victory. Meanwhile, passion means to act, and action is the basis of defeat."

KING HSIANG OF LIANG asked Mencius, "How can the kingdom be pacified?" Mencius answered, "The kingdom can be pacified by uniting it." King Hsiang asked, "But who can unite it?" Mencius answered, "One who does not delight in killing others can unite it" (*Mencius*: 1A.6).

LI JUNG says, "The ancients used weapons with compassion. They honored them for their virtue and disdained them as tools. Once the enemy was defeated, the general put on plain, undyed clothes, presided over a funeral ceremony, and received the mourners."

In the first line, I have followed the arguments of Wang Nien-sun and Cheng Liang-shu in reading *chia* (fine), which precedes *ping* (weapons) in the standard editions, as a mistake for the grammatical particle *wei*, which carries no meaning, only emphasis. Lines two and three also appear in verse 24, although my translation of them there is not the same. The first three lines are missing from the Kuotien texts, as is line seven. For line ten, I have followed the wording of the Fuyi and Mawangtui texts, which the standard versions render "victory is not praised."

32

道恆無名。朴雖小。天下莫能臣。

侯王若能守之。萬物將自賓。天地相合。

以渝甘露。民莫之令。而自均焉。始制有名。

名亦既有。夫亦將知止。知止所以不殆。

譬道之在天下也。猶小浴之於江海也。

The Tao remains unnamed
simple and though small
no one can command it
if a lord upheld it
the world would be his guest
when Heaven joins with Earth
they bestow sweet dew
no one gives the order
it comes down to all
the first distinction gives us names
once we have a name
we should know restraint
who knows restraint avoids trouble
to picture the Tao in the world
imagine a stream and the sea

WANG P'ANG says, "The Tao has no body. How could it have a name?"

HO-SHANG KUNG says, "We call it 'simple' because it hasn't been cut or polished. We call it 'small' because it's faint and infinitesimal. Those who can see what is small and hold on to it are rare indeed."

CHIAO HUNG says, "'Simple' means the natural state. When it expands, it's everywhere. When it contracts, it isn't as big as the tip of a hair. Hence, even though it's small, it's beyond anyone's command."

WANG PI says, "If people embrace the simple and work without effort and don't burden their true nature with material goods or injure their spirit with desires, all things will come to them on their own, and they will discover the Tao by themselves. To discover the Tao, nothing is better than embracing simplicity."

JEN FA-JUNG says, "In terms of practice, if people can be serene and natural, free themselves from desire, and put their minds at rest, their *yin* and *yang* breaths will come together on their own and penetrate every artery and organ. Inside their mouths, the saliva of sweet dew will appear spontaneously and nourish their whole body."

LU HUI-CH'ING says, "When a ruler acts, the first thing he does is institute names."

HSUN-TZU says, "Now that the sages are gone, names and reality have become confused" (*Hsuntzu: 2*).

TE-CH'ING says, "What is simple has no name. Once we make something, we give it a name. But name gives rise to name. Where does it end? Hence, Lao-tzu tells us to stop chasing names."

LI JUNG says, "The child who depends on its mother suffers no harm. Those who depend on the Tao encounter no trouble."

WU CH'ENG says, "The Tao has no name, but as Virtue it does. Thus, from nothing we get something. But Virtue is not far from the Tao. If we stop there, we can still go from something back to nothing and return to the Tao. Thus, the Tao is like the sea, and Virtue is like a stream, flowing back into the Tao."

LI HSI-CHAI says, "Although Heaven and Earth are high and low, they join together and send down sweet dew. No one makes them do so. And there is no one who does not benefit. Although the Tao separates into things, and each thing has its name, the Tao never abandons anything. Thus, the breath of rivers eventually reaches the sea, and the breath of the sea eventually reaches rivers."

LAO-TZU says, "The reason the sea can govern a hundred rivers / is because it has mastered being lower" (*Taoteching: 66*).

The phrase *kan-lu,* "sweet dew," also refers to the saliva produced during meditation by pressing the tongue against the roof of the mouth. Line thirteen also appears in verse 44. In the last line, I've followed the Kuotien and Mawangtui texts in reading *hsiao-ku* (small valley; hence stream) in place of the standard *ch'uan-ku* (river valley), and I've also read *yu* (valley) as a substitute for the graphically similar *hsi* (stream).

33

知人者智。自知者明。
勝人者有力。自勝者強。
知足者富。強行者有志。
不失其所者久。
死而不亡者壽。

Those who know others are perceptive
those who know themselves are wise
those who conquer others are forceful
those who conquer themselves are strong
those who know contentment are wealthy
those who strive hard are resolved
those who don't lose their place endure
those who aren't affected by death live long

SU CH'E says, "Perception means to distinguish. Wisdom means to remove obstructions. As long as our distinguishing mind is present, we can only know others, but not ourselves."

LI HSI-CHAI says, "Perception is external knowledge. Wisdom is internal knowledge. Force is external control. Strength is internal control. Perception and force mislead us. Wisdom and strength are true. They are the doors to the Tao."

HO-SHANG KUNG says, "If someone can conquer others, it is only by using force. If someone can conquer their own desires, no one in the world can compete with them. Hence, we call them strong."

SUNG CH'ANG-HSING says, "The strength of those who conquer themselves is of ten kinds: the strength of faith, the strength of charity, the strength of morality, the strength of devotion, the strength of meditation, the strength of concentration, the strength of illumination, the strength of wisdom, the strength of the Way, and the strength of Virtue." (Note the similarity of this list to Buddhism's *paramitas,* or perfections)

WU CH'ENG says, "Elsewhere, Lao-tzu extols simplemindedness and weakness over wisdom and strength. Why then does he extol wisdom and strength here? Wisdom and strength are for dealing with the inside. Simplemindedness and weakness are for dealing with the outside."

WANG P'ANG says, "The natural endowment of all beings is complete in itself. Poverty does not reduce it. Wealth does not enlarge it. But fools abandon this treasure to chase trash. Those who know contentment pay the world no heed. This is true wealth. Mencius said, 'The ten thousand things are all within us' (*Mencius*: 7A.4). How could we not be wealthy?"

TS'AO TAO-CH'UNG says, "Although the Great Way might be far off, if we persevere without pause, we advance. We get closer and closer, until suddenly we become one with the Way. Whoever has a goal can do anything. Outside, be content with your lot. Inside, focus on the Way. Those who do this cannot help but live long."

WANG PI says, "Those who strive with devotion reach their goal. Those who examine themselves and work within their capacity don't lose their place and are able to endure. Although we die, the Tao that gave us life doesn't perish. Our body disappears, but the Tao remains. If our body continued to survive, would the Tao not end?"

TE-CH'ING says, "Our 'place' is like the position of the North Star. It refers to our nature."

CONFUCIUS says, "Those who govern with Virtue are like the North Star, which remains in its place, while the myriad stars revolve around it" (*Lunyu*: 2.1).

LU NUNG-SHIH says, "Before we distinguish life and death, they share the same form, the ten thousand things dwell in the same house. Our body is like the shell of a cicada or the skin of a snake: a temporary lodging. The shell crumbles but not the cicada. The skin decays but not the snake. We all have something real that survives death."

KUMARAJIVA says, "Not to live in living is to endure. Not to die in dying is to live long."

Although the *ch'iang-hsing* (striving hard) of line six seems at odds with Lao-tzu's dictum of *wu-wei*, "doing nothing/effortlessness," commentators are agreed that here it refers to inner cultivation and not to the pursuit of worldly goals. This verse is absent from the Kuotien texts.

34

是 而 則 而 道
以 不 恆 不 汎
聖 為 無 辭 兮
人 大 欲 。 。
終 。 。 成 其
不 故 可 功 可
為 能 名 遂 左
大 成 於 事 右
。 其 小 。 。
大 。 而 萬
。 萬 不 物
物 名 恃
歸 有 之
焉 。 以
。 生
。

The Tao drifts
it can go left or right
everything lives by its grace
but it doesn't speak
when its work succeeds
it makes no claim
it has no desires
shall we call it small
everything turns to it
but it wields no control
shall we call it great
it's because sages never act great
they can thus achieve great things

HSUAN-TSUNG says, "To drift means to be unrestrained. The Tao is neither *yin* nor *yang*, weak nor strong. Unrestrained, it can respond to all things and in any direction. It isn't one-sided. As Chuang-tzu says, 'The Tao has no borders' [*Chuangtzu*: 2.5]."

CHUANG-TZU says, "Those who are skilled toil, and those who are clever worry. Meanwhile, those who do not possess such abilities seek nothing and yet eat their fill. They drift through life like unmoored boats" (*Chuangtzu*: 32.1).

WANG PI says, "The Tao drifts everywhere. It can go left or right. It can go up or down. Wherever we turn, it's there for us to use."

LI HSI-CHAI says, "The Great Way is a watery expanse that extends to the eight horizons. But when we use it, it's as close as our left or right hand. There is nothing that doesn't depend on it for life, and yet it never speaks of its power. There is nothing that doesn't happen without its help, and yet it never mentions its achievements."

SUNG CH'ANG-HSING says, "Outside of the Tao there are no things. Outside of things there is no Tao. The Tao gives birth to things, just as wind creates movement or water creates waves."

TS'AO TAO-CH'UNG says, "Although living things might be infinite in number, the Tao creates them all through the mystery of doing nothing. It doesn't mind making so many. And it creates them without thinking about its power."

WANG P'ANG says, "When the Tao becomes small, it doesn't stop being great. And when it becomes great, it doesn't stop being small. But all we see are its traces. In reality, it is neither small nor great. It can't be described. It can only be known."

CH'ENG HSUAN-YING says, "The Tao produces all things, and all things turn to it. It's like the sea. All streams empty into it, and yet it doesn't control them."

Commenting on lines eight and eleven, WU CH'ENG says, "Even though there are no question indicators, these are questions and not statements, just as in verse 10. If we can call something great, it isn't the Tao."

SU CH'E says, "Those who are great and think themselves great are small."

LU HUI-CH'ING says, "The Tao hides in what has no name, and sages embody it through what has no name. They don't consider themselves great, and yet no one is greater, for they can go left or right. Hence, they are neither small nor great. And because they are neither small nor great, they can do great things."

Who says the Tao doesn't speak? This verse is not present in the Kuotien texts, and the Mawangtui texts omit lines three and four. Following line six, the standard editions have two additional lines: "it cares for all things / yet it wields no control." But this anticipates line ten, and I have gone along with the Mawangtui texts in not including them. For the last two lines, I have followed the standard editions, while the Mawangtui texts have the more convoluted and redundant "therefore sages can do great things / because they do not act great / they thus can do great things."

35

執大象。天下往。往而不害。安平泰。樂與餌。過客止。故道之出言。淡乎其無味。視之不足見。聽之不足聞。用之不可既。

Hold up the Great Image
and the world will come
and be beyond harm
safe and serene and at peace
fine food and song
don't detain guests long
thus the Tao speaks
plain words that make no sense
we look but don't see it
we listen but don't hear it
yet we use it without end

CH'ENG HSUAN-YING says, "Here 'hold' means to hold without holding, to hold what cannot be held."

HUANG YUAN-CHI says, "The Great Image is the Great Way, which gives birth to Heaven and Earth and all creatures. It is called 'great' because it encompasses everything."

LI JUNG says, "The Great Image has no form. What has no form is the great and empty Way. To 'hold' means to focus or to keep. Those who can keep their body in the realm of Dark Virtue and focus their mind on the gate of Hidden Serenity possess the Way. All things come to them. Clouds appear, and all creatures are refreshed. Rain pours down, and all plants are nourished. And these blessings come from such a subtle thing."

WU CH'ENG says, "To come to no harm means to be protected. But when people turn to sages, sages use no protection to protect them. If they protected people with protection, protection and harm would both exist. But by protecting people with no protection, people are always protected and kept from harm."

LU TUNG-PIN says, "Unharmed, our spirit is safe. Unharmed, our breath is serene. Unharmed, our nature is at peace."

TE-CH'ING says, "Sages rule the world through selflessness. All things come to them because they are one with all things. And while they forget themselves in others, others forget themselves in them. Thus, all things find their place, and there are none that are not at peace."

CHANG TAO-LING says, "What the Tao says is the opposite of the mundane or the clever. Most people find it completely senseless. But within its senselessness, there is great sense. This is what sages savor. The Tao prefers simplicity of form and a minimum of expression. Hence, it is hard to see and hard to hear and also hard to follow. But those who can follow it and use it enjoy limitless blessings."

CHUANG-TZU says, "A great person's words are plain like water. A small person's words are sweet like wine. The plainness of a great person brings people closer, while the sweetness of a small person drives them apart. Those who come together for no reason, separate for no reason" (*Chuangtzu*: 20.5).

SU CH'E says, "Banquets and entertainment might detain visitors, but sooner or later the food runs out, the music ends, and visitors leave. If someone entertained the world with the Great Image, no one would know how to love it, much less hate it. Although it has no taste, shape, or sound with which to please people, those who use it can never exhaust it."

HO-SHANG KUNG says, "If someone used the Tao to govern the country, the country would be rich, and the people would be prosperous. If someone used it to cultivate themselves, there would be no limit to the length of their life."

The Great Image is Te, or Virtue, the manifestation of the Tao. I have followed the Kuotien and Mawangtui texts in adding *ku* (thus) to line seven. Lines nine and ten are also echoed in verse 14: "We look but don't see it / and call it indistinct / we listen but don't hear it / and call it faint."

36

將欲歙之。必故張之。將欲弱之。必故強之。將欲廢之。必故興之。將欲奪之。必故予之。是謂微明。柔弱勝強。魚不可脫於淵。邦之利器。不可以示人。

What you would shorten
you first should lengthen
what you would weaken
you first should strengthen
what you would topple
you first should raise
what you would take
you first should give
this is called hiding the light
the weak conquering the strong
fish can't survive out of the depths
a state's greatest weapon
isn't meant to be shown

TE-CH'ING says, "Once things reach their limit, they go the other way. Hence, lengthening is a portent of shortening. Strengthening is the onset of weakening. Raising is the beginning of toppling. Giving is the start of taking. This is the natural order for Heaven as well as for Humankind. Thus, to hide the light means the weak conquer the strong. Weakness is the greatest weapon of the state. But rulers must not show it to their people. Deep water is the best place for a fish. But once it is exposed to the air, a fish is completely helpless. And once rulers show weakness, they attract enemies and shame."

LU HUI-CH'ING says, "To perceive shortening in lengthening, weakening in strengthening, toppling in raising, taking in giving, how could anyone do this if not through the deepest insight? This is the hidden light. Moreover, what causes things to be shortened or lengthened, weakened or strengthened, toppled or raised, taken or given is invisible and weak. While what is shortened or lengthened, weakened or strengthened, toppled or raised, taken or given is visible and strong. Thus, the weak conquer the strong. People should not abandon weakness, just as fish should not leave the depths. When fish leave the depths, they are caught. When people abandon weakness, they join the league of the dead."

WU CH'ENG says, "'Hiding the light' is the same as 'cloaking the light.'" (See verse 27.)

SUNG CH'ANG-HSING says, "According to the way of the world, the weak don't conquer the strong. But Lao-tzu's point is that the weak can conquer the strong by letting the strong do what they want until they become exhausted and thus weak. Those who cultivate the Tao speak softly and act with care. They don't argue about right or wrong, better or worse. They understand the harmony of Heaven and Earth, the Way of emptiness and stillness, and become adept at using the hidden light."

CHANG TAO-LING says, "The Tao is like water. People are like fish."

CHUANG-TZU says, "The sage is the world's greatest weapon but not one that is known to the world" (*Chuangtzu*: 10.3).

HAN FEI says, "Rewards and punishments are the state's greatest weapon."

I've added Han Fei's comment here because the strong still rule the day. Although the differences among editions are not significant, both Mawangtui versions of lines five and six abandon the rhyme. I have followed the Fuyi and Wangpi texts here, switching, however, to the Mawangtui versions of line ten, which the Fuyi and Wangpi editions expand into two lines: "the soft conquer the hard / the weak conquer the strong." The copyist was probably thinking ahead to verse 78, where this couplet does, in fact, occur. Note that the appearance of *pang* (state) in line twelve of the Fuyi edition and Mawangtui A suggests that both were copied before Liu Pang became emperor in 206 B.C., and the use of his name was forbidden. On the other hand, Mawangtui B has *kuo* (country), suggesting that it was copied after 206 B.C.

37

道恆無為。而無不為。俟王若能守之。萬物將自化。化而欲作。吾將鎮之。以無名之朴。鎮之以無名之朴。夫將不欲。不欲以靜。天下將自正。

The Tao makes no effort at all
yet there is nothing it doesn't do
if a ruler could uphold it
the people by themselves would change
and changing if their desires stirred
he could make them still
with simplicity that has no name
and stilled by nameless simplicity
they would not desire
and not desiring be at peace
the world would fix itself

CHUANG-TZU says, "The ancients ruled the world by doing nothing. This is the Virtue of Heaven. Heaven moves without moving" (*Chuangtzu*: 12.1).

WU CH'ENG says, "The Tao's lack of effort is ancient and eternal and not simply temporary. Although it makes no effort, it does everything it should do. If rulers could uphold this Tao of effortlessness, without consciously thinking about changing others, others would change by themselves."

LAO-TZU says, "I make no effort / and the people transform themselves" (*Taoteching*: 57).

TE-CH'ING says, "If nobles and kings could only uphold the Tao, all creatures would change by themselves without thinking about changing. This is the effect of upholding the Tao. When creatures first change, their desires disappear. But before long, their trust fades and feelings well up and begin to flow until desires reappear. When this occurs, those who are adept at saving others must block the source of desire with nameless simplicity."

HO-SHANG KUNG says, "'Nameless simplicity' refers to the Tao, which all creatures use to transform themselves and which nobles and kings use to pacify those who engage in cleverness and deceit."

CH'ENG HSUAN-YING says, "When people first change and begin to cultivate the Tao, they think about reaching a goal. Once this desire arises, it must be stilled with the Tao's nameless simplicity."

SU CH'E says, "Sages have no thought of embracing simplicity, nor do they show any sign of doing so. If the thought of becoming simple existed in their hearts, they would miss the mark completely."

HSUAN-TSUNG says, "Once rulers use nameless simplicity to still the desires of the people, they must then give it up so that the people don't follow its tracks and once again enter the realm of action. Once our illness is cured, we put away the medicine. Once we are across the river, we leave the boat behind. And once we are free of desire, we must also forget the desire to be free of desire. Serene and at peace, the ruler does nothing, while the world takes care of itself."

SUNG CH'ANG-HSING says, "Other creatures follow their natures without creating chaos or disaster. They change by themselves without seeking change. People, meanwhile, race through the realm of existence and never know a quiet moment. They abandon their original innocence and don't practice the true Tao of doing nothing. They don't care about their lives, until one day they offend and retribution arrives."

Name takes sides. Complexity limits options. Hence, those who uphold nameless simplicity don't take sides and keep their options open. The first two lines appear as one line in verse 48 (line five). In place of the first line, the Mawangtui texts have: "The Tao has no name at all." But this must be an interpolation from verse 32 and appears in no other edition. The Kuotien texts have the same first line but omit the second line, as do the Mawangtui texts. In lines nine and ten, the Mawangtui texts replace *yu* (desire) with *ju* (shame). Although I haven't followed that emendation, I have followed the Mawangtui repetition of *chen-chih-yi* (stilled by) at the beginning of line eight. The Kuotien texts omit line eight and in lines nine and ten replace *pu-yu* (no desire) with *chih-tsu* (know when they have enough). In the last line, the Mawangtui texts replace *t'ien-hsia* (the world) with *t'ien-ti* (heaven and earth), while the Kuotien texts have *wan-wu* (all things).

38

是以大丈居其厚而不居其薄。居其實而不居其華。故去彼取此。

夫禮者忠信之薄。而亂之首。前識者道之華。而愚之始。

則攘臂而扔之。故失道而後德。失德而後仁。失仁而後義。失義而後禮。

上仁為之。而無以為。上義為之。而有以為。上禮為之。而莫之應。

上德不德。是以有德。下德不失德。是以無德。上德無為。而無以為。

Higher Virtue isn't virtuous
thus it possesses virtue
Lower Virtue isn't without virtue
thus it possesses no virtue
Higher Virtue involves no effort
or the thought of effort
Higher Kindness involves effort
but not the thought of effort
Higher Justice involves effort
and the thought of effort
Higher Ritual involves effort
and should it meet with no response
then it threatens and compels
virtue appears when the Way is lost
kindness appears when virtue is lost
justice appears when kindness is lost
ritual appears when justice is lost
ritual marks the waning of belief
and the onset of confusion
augury is the flower of the Way
and beginning of delusion
thus the great choose thick over thin
the fruit over the flower
thus they pick this over that

HAN FEI says, "Virtue is the Tao at work."

WANG PI says, "Those who possess Higher Virtue use nothing but the Tao. They possess virtue, but they don't give it a name."

YEN TSUN says, "Those who embody the Way are empty and effortless, yet they lead all creatures to the Way. Those who embody virtue are faultless and responsive and ready to do anything. Those who embody kindness show love for all creatures without restriction. Those who embody justice deal with things by matching name with reality. Those who embody ritual are humble and put harmony first. These five are the footprints of the Tao. They are not the ultimate goal. The ultimate goal is not one, much less five."

WANG P'ANG says, "Kindness is another name for virtue. It differs, though, from virtue because it involves effort. The kindness of sages, however, does not go beyond fulfilling their nature. They aren't interested in effort. Hence, they don't think about it."

LU HUI-CH'ING says, "Higher Kindness is kindness without effort to be kind. Kindness is simply a gift. Justice is concerned with the appropriateness of the gift. Ritual is concerned with repayment. When ritual appears, belief disappears and confusion arises."

SU CH'E says, "These are the means whereby sages help the people to safety. When the people don't respond, sages threaten and force them. If they still don't respond, sages turn to law and punishment."

FAN YING-YUAN says, "'Augury' means to see the future. Those in charge of rituals think they can see the future and devise formulas for human action, but they thus cause people to trade the spirit for the letter."

WU CH'ENG says, "The Tao is like a fruit. Hanging from a tree, it contains the power of life, but its womb is hidden. Once it falls, it puts forth virtue as its root, kindness as its stem, justice as its branches, ritual as its leaves, and knowledge as its flower. All of these come from the Tao. 'That' refers to the flower. 'This' refers to the fruit. Those who embody the Tao choose the fruit over the flower."

And yet the plastic flowers of civilization still deck a billion altars. After line six, the Wangpi and Fuyi editions add: "Lower Virtue involves effort / but not the thought of effort." But this is the same description of Higher Kindness. I've followed the Mawangtui texts, which don't include this line. The above categories (Higher Virtue, etc.) also appear as chapter titles in the *Wentzu,* a Taoist text ascribed to a student of Lao-tzu and fragments of which have been found dating back to the third century B.C.

39

昔之得一者。天得一以清。地得一以寧。神得一以靈。谷得一以盈。
侯王得一以為天下正。其致之謂。天無已清將恐裂。地無已寧將恐發。
神無已靈將恐歇。谷無已盈將恐竭。侯王無已貴而高將恐蹶。
故必貴以賤為本。必高以下為基。是以侯王自稱。孤寡不穀。
此其賤之本歟非也。故致數輿無輿。不欲琭琭如玉。落落如石。

Of those that became one in the past
Heaven became one and was clear
Earth became one and was still
spirits became one and were active
valleys became one and were full
kings became one and ruled the world
but from this we can infer
Heaven would crack if it were always clear
Earth would crumble if it were always still
spirits would dissipate if they were always active
valleys would dry up if they were always full
kings would fall if they were always high and noble
for the noble is based on the humble
and the high is founded on the low
thus do kings refer to themselves
as orphaned widowed and destitute
but this isn't the basis of humility
counting a carriage as no carriage at all
not wanting to clink like jade
they clunk like rocks

WANG PI says, "One is the beginning of numbers and the end of things. All things become complete when they become one. But once they become complete, they leave oneness behind and focus on being complete. And by focusing on being complete, they lose their mother. Hence, they crack, they crumble, they dissipate, they dry up, and they fall. As long as they have their mother, they can preserve their form. But their mother has no form."

HO-SHANG KUNG says, "It's because Heaven becomes one that it graces the sky with constellations and light. It's because Earth becomes one that it remains still and immovable. It's because spirits become one that they change shape without becoming visible. It's because valleys become one that they never stop filling up. It's because kings become one that they pacify the world. But Heaven must move between *yin* and *yang*, between night and day. It can't only be clear and bright. Earth must include high and low, hard and soft, and the fivefold stages of breath. It can't only be still. Spirits must have periods of quiescence. They can't only be active. Valleys must also be empty and dry. They can't only be full. And kings must humble themselves and never stop seeking worthy people to assist them. They can't only lord it over others. If they do, they fall from power and lose their thrones."

CHENG LIANG-SHU says, "In ancient times, kings used carriages as metaphors for the wealth and size of their kingdoms. To refer to one's carriages as no carriages was an expression of self-deprecation."

SU CH'E says, "Oneness dwells in the noble, but it is not noble. Oneness dwells in the humble, but it is not humble. Oneness is not like the luster of jade (so noble it cannot be humble) or the coarseness of rock (so humble it cannot be noble)."

One is the number between zero and two. Between lines five and six, the Fuyi and Wangpi editions add the line: "all creatures became one and were alive." And between lines eleven and twelve they add: "creatures would die if they were always alive." However, neither line appears in the Yen Tsun or Mawangtui texts, and I have not included them. In line seven, I have also chosen the Mawangtui *wei* (mean) over the standard *yi* (one). I have used the Mawangtui texts again for lines eight through twelve, where they have *wu-yi* (without stop/always) in place of the usual *wu-yi* (without means). This usage is also supported by Ho-shang Kung. For line eighteen, I have turned to the Mawangtui texts once more, along with Cheng Liang-shu's interpretation of it. The Fuyi and standard editions have: "counting their fame as no fame at all."

40

有生于無。
天下之物生于有。
弱者道之用。
反者道之動。

The Tao moves the other way
the Tao works through weakness
the things of this world come from something
something comes from nothing

LIU CH'EN-WENG says, "Once things reach their limit, they have to go back the other way."

WEI YUAN says, "The Tao moves contrary to how most people look at things."

CH'AO CHIH-CHIEN says, "To go back the other way means to return to the root. Those who cultivate the Tao ignore the twigs and seek the root. This is the movement of the Tao: to return to where the mind is still and empty and actions soft and weak. The Tao, however, does not actually come or go. It never leaves. Hence, it cannot return. Only what has form returns. 'Something' refers to breath. Before things have form they have breath. Heaven and Earth and the ten thousand things are born from breath. Hence, they all come from something. 'Nothing' refers to the Tao. Breath comes from the Tao. Hence, it comes from nothing. This is the movement of the Tao."

WANG AN-SHIH says, "The reason the Tao works through weakness is because it is empty. We see it in Heaven blowing through the great void. We see it in Earth sinking into the deepest depths."

TE-CH'ING says, "People only know the work of working. They don't know that the work of not working is the greatest work of all. They only know that everything comes from something. They don't know that something comes from nothing. If they knew that something came from nothing, they would no longer enslave themselves to things. They would turn, instead, to the Tao and concentrate on their spirit."

HO-SHANG KUNG says, "The ten thousand things all come from Heaven and Earth. Heaven and Earth have position and form. Hence, we say things come from something. The light and spirit of Heaven and Earth, the flight of insects, the movement of worms, these all come from the Tao. The Tao has no form. Hence, we say things come from nothing. This means the root comes before the flower, weakness comes before strength, humility comes before conceit."

LI JUNG says, "'Something' refers to Heaven and Earth. Through the protection of Heaven and the support of Earth, all things come into being. 'Nothing' refers to the Tao. The Tao is formless and empty, and yet it gives birth to Heaven and Earth. Thus, it is said, 'Emptiness is the root of Heaven and Earth. Nothingness is the source of all things.' Those who lose the Tao don't realize where things come from."

SU CH'E says, "As for 'the things of this world,' I have heard of a mother giving birth to a child. But I have never heard of a child giving birth to its mother."

WANG PI says, "Everything in the world comes from being, and being comes from nonbeing. If you would reach perfect being, you have to go back to nonbeing."

HUANG YUAN-CHI says, "Those who cultivate the Way should act with humility and harmony. The slightest carelessness, any action at all, can destroy everything. Those who cultivate Virtue look to themselves for the truth, not to the words of others. For those who understand that what moves them is also the source of their lives, the pill of immortality is not somewhere outside."

The moon can't keep up with the sun, but as it gets farther and farther behind, the darkness of nothing gives rise to the light of something. In line three, some editions add *wan* (ten thousand) to *wu* (things). The Mawangtui texts reverse the order of verses 40 and 41. Also, some commentators read 40 as a continuation of 39, while others combine it with 41. *Wentzu: 1* provides a slightly different version of the first two lines: "The Tao works through weakness / the Tao keeps moving the other way." The Kuotien texts do not have the word *yu* (something) in line four. Scholars disagree as to whether this was intentional or simply a copyist error.

41

上士聞道。勤而行之。中士聞道。若存若亡。下士聞道。
大笑之。不笑。不足以為道。是以建言有之曰。明道若昧。
進道若退。夷道若類。上德若谷。大白若黷。廣德不足。
建德若偷。質真若渝。大方無隅。大器免成。
大象無形。道隱無名。夫唯道。善始且善成。

When superior people hear of the Way
they follow it with devotion
when average people hear of the Way
they wonder if it exists
when inferior people hear of the Way
they laugh out loud
if they didn't laugh
it wouldn't be the Way
hence these sayings arose
the brightest path seems dark
the path leading forward seems backward
the smoothest path seems rough
the highest virtue low
the whitest white pitch-black
the greatest virtue wanting
the staunchest virtue timid
the truest truth uncertain
the perfect square without corners
the perfect tool without uses
the perfect sound hushed
the perfect image without form
for the Tao is hidden and nameless
but because it's the Tao
it knows how to start and how to finish

CONFUCIUS says, "To hear of the Tao in the morning is to die content by night-fall" (*Lunyu: 4.8*).

LI HSI-CHAI says, "When great people hear of the Tao, even if others laugh at them, they can't keep them from practicing it. When average people hear of the Tao, even if they don't disbelieve it, they can't free themselves of doubts. When inferior people hear of the Tao, even the ancient sages can't keep them from laughing. Everyone in the world thinks existence is real. Who wouldn't shake their head and laugh if they were told that existence wasn't real and that non-existence was?"

TE-CH'ING says, "The Tao is not what people expect. Hence, the ancients created these twelve sayings, which Lao-tzu quotes to make clear that the Tao has two sides."

SU CH'E says, "These twelve sayings refer to the Tao as it appears to us. Wherever we look, we see its examples. The Tao as a whole, however, is hidden in namelessness."

LI JUNG says, "The true Tao is neither fast nor slow, clear nor obscure. It has no appearance, no sound, no form, and no name. But although it has no name, it can take any name."

LU HUI-CH'ING says, "Name and reality are often at odds. The reality of the Tao remains hidden in no name."

LU HSI-SHENG says, "Tools are limited to the realm of form. The Tao is beyond the realm of form."

YEN TSUN says, "The quail runs and flies all day but never far from an over-grown field. The swan flies a thousand miles but never far from a pond. The phoenix, meanwhile, soars into the empyrean vault and thinks it too confining. Where dragons dwell, small fish swim past. Where great birds and beasts live, dogs and chickens don't go."

THE *CHANKUOTSE* says, "Those who know how to start don't always know how to finish" (31).

In line fourteen, my reading of *ju* (pitch-black) instead of the usual *ju* (disgrace) is based on the Fuyi edition. In line sixteen, I have followed Kao Heng in reading *t'ou* (steal) as a loan for *ju* (timid). In the last line, I have gone along with Mawangtui B in reading *shih* (start) instead of the standard, and yet puzzling, *tai* (bestow). This verse is present in the Kuotien texts, but in those lines where it is readable, it doesn't introduce any significant variations.

42

道生一。一生二。二生三。三生萬物。
萬物負陰。而抱陽。中氣以為和。天下之所惡。
唯孤寡不穀。而王公以自名。故物或損之而益。
或益之而損。故人之所教。我亦教之。
強梁者不得其死。吾將以為教父。

The Tao gives birth to one
one gives birth to two
two gives birth to three
three gives birth to ten thousand things
ten thousand things with *yin* at their backs
yang in their embrace
and breath between for harmony
what the world hates
to be orphaned widowed or destitute
kings use for their titles
thus some gain by losing
others lose by gaining
what others teach
I teach too
tyrants never choose their death
this becomes my teacher

HO-SHANG KUNG says, "The Tao gives birth to the beginning. One gives birth to *yin* and *yang*. *Yin* and *yang* give birth to the breath between them, the mixture of clear and turbid. These three breaths divide themselves into Heaven, Earth, and Humankind and together give birth to the ten thousand things. These elemental breaths are what keep the ten thousand things relaxed and balanced. The organs in our chest, the marrow in our bones, the hollow spaces inside plants all allow these breaths passage and make long life possible."

LI HSI-CHAI says, "The *yang* we embrace is one. The *yin* we turn away from is two. Where *yin* and *yang* meet and merge is three."

LU HUI-CH'ING says, "Dark and unfathomable is *yin*. Bright and perceptible is *yang*. As soon as we are born, we all turn our back on the dark and unfathomable *yin* and turn toward the bright and perceptible *yang*. Fortunately, we keep ourselves in harmony with the breath between them."

THE *YUNCHI CHICHIEN* says, "When breath is pure, it becomes Heaven. When it becomes turgid, it becomes Earth. And the mixture of the breath between them becomes Humankind."

TE-CH'ING says, "To call oneself 'orphaned,' 'widowed,' or 'destitute' is to use a title of self-effacement. Rulers who are not self-effacing are not looked up to by the world. Thus, by losing, they gain. Rulers who are only aware of themselves might possess the world, but the world rebels against them. Thus, by gaining, they lose. We all share this Tao, but we don't know it except through instruction. What others teach, Lao-tzu also teaches. But Lao-tzu surpasses others in teaching us to reduce our desires and to be humble, to practice the virtue of harmony, and to let this be our teacher."

CHIAO HUNG says, "Those who love victory make enemies. The ancients taught this, and so does Lao-tzu. But Lao-tzu goes further and calls this his own 'teacher.'"

KAO HENG says, "According to the *Shuoyuan* (10.25), 'Tyrants never choose their death' was an ancient saying, which Confucius attributed to the *Chinjenming*. This is what Lao-tzu refers to when he says 'what others teach.'"

WANG P'ANG says, "Whatever contains the truth can be our teacher. Although tyrants kill others and are the most hated of creatures, we can learn the principle of creation and destruction from them."

In line seven I have followed Mawangtui A, which has *chung* (between) in place of the usual *ch'ung* (empty). Lines nine and ten are echoed in verse 39. In line thirteen, I have incorporated *ku* (thus) from Mawangtui A. And in line fourteen, several Tunhuang copies add *yi* (justly), while Mawangtui A has *yi* (thoughtfully). Both are apparently mistakes for the graphically similar *wo* (I), which appears in the Fuyi, Wangpi, and other standard editions. This verse is not present in the Kuotien texts.

43

天下希能及之矣。
不言之教。無為之益。
吾是以知無為之有益。
無有入於無間。
天下之至柔。馳騁於天下之至堅。

The weakest thing in the world
overcomes the strongest thing in the world
what doesn't exist finds room where there's none
thus we know help comes with no effort
wordless instruction
effortless help
few in the world can match this

LAO-TZU says, "Nothing in the world is weaker than water / but against the hard and the strong / nothing outdoes it" (*Taoteching*: 78).

WANG TAO says, "Eight feet of water can float a thousand-ton ship. Six feet of leather can control a thousand-mile horse. Thus does the weak excel the strong. Sunlight has no substance, yet it can fill a dark room. Thus, what doesn't exist enters what has no cracks."

Concerning the first two lines, HUAI-NAN-TZU says, "The light of the sun shines across the Four Seas but cannot penetrate a closed door or a covered window. While the light of the spirit reaches everywhere and nourishes everything." Concerning the second couplet, he says, "Illumination once asked Nonexistence if it actually existed or not. Nonexistence made no response. Unable to perceive any sign of its existence, Illumination sighed and said, 'I, too, do not exist, but I cannot equal the nonexistence of Nonexistence'" (*Huainantzu*: 12).

LI HSI-CHAI says, "Things are not actually things. What we call 'strong' is a fiction. Once it reaches its limit, it returns to nothing. Thus, the weakest thing in the world is able to overcome the strongest thing in the world. Or do you think the reality of nonexistence cannot break through the fiction of existence?"

WANG PI says, "There is nothing breath cannot enter and nothing water cannot penetrate. What does not exist cannot be exhausted. And what is perfectly weak cannot be broken. From this we can infer the benefit of no effort."

SU CH'E says, "If we control the strong with the strong, one will break, or the other will shatter. But if we control the strong with the weak, the weak will not be exhausted, and the strong will not be damaged. Water is like this. If we use existence to enter existence, neither is able to withstand the other. But if we use nonexistence to enter existence, the former will not strain itself, while the latter will remain unaware. Spirits are like this."

HO-SHANG KUNG says, "'What doesn't exist' refers to the Tao. The Tao has no form or substance. Hence, it can come and go, even where there is not any space. It can fill the spirit and help all creatures. We don't see it do anything, and yet the ten thousand things are transformed and completed. Thus, we realize the benefit to Humankind of no effort. Imitating the Tao, we don't speak. We follow it with our bodies. Imitating the Tao, we don't act. We care for ourselves, and our spirits prosper. We care for our country, and the people flourish. And we do these things without effort or trouble. But few can match the Tao in caring for things by doing nothing. Lao-tzu's final 'in the world' refers to rulers."

YEN TSUN says, "Action is the beginning of chaos. Stillness is the origin of order. Speech is the door of misfortune. Silence is the gate of blessing."

TE-CH'ING says, "Words mean traces. Traces mean knowledge. Knowledge means presumption. Presumption means involvement. And involvement means failure."

One day CONFUCIUS said, "I would rather not speak." Tzu-kung asked, "If you do not speak, what will we have to record?" Confucius replied, "Does Heaven speak? The seasons travel their course, and creatures all flourish. What does Heaven say?" (*Lunyu*: 17.19).

This verse does not appear in the Kuotien texts, and there are no significant textual issues in those editions where it does appear.

44

名與身。孰親。身與貨。孰多。得與亡。
孰病。甚愛。必大費。多藏。必厚亡。
故知足。不辱。知止。不殆。可以長久。

Which is more vital
fame or health
which is more precious
health or wealth
which is more harmful
loss or gain
the deeper the love
the higher the cost
the bigger the treasure
the greater the loss
who knows contentment
thus suffers no shame
and who knows restraint
encounters no trouble
while enjoying a long life

HUANG MAO-TS'AI says, "What the world calls fame is something external. And yet people abandon their bodies to fight for it. What the world calls wealth is unpredictable. And yet people sacrifice their bodies to possess it. How can they know what is vital or precious? Even if they succeed, it's at the cost of their health."

SSU-MA KUANG says, "Which is more harmful: to gain wealth and fame and lose one's health or to gain one's health and lose wealth and fame?"

LU HUI-CH'ING says, "Heroes seek fame and merchants seek wealth, even to the point of giving up their lives. The first love fame because they want to glorify themselves. But the more they love fame, the more they lose what they would really glorify. Hence, the cost is high. The second amass wealth because they want to enrich themselves. But the more wealth they amass, the more they harm what they would truly enrich. Hence, the loss is great. Meanwhile, those who cultivate Virtue know the most vital thing is within themselves. Thus, they seek no fame and suffer no disgrace. They know the most precious thing is within themselves. Thus, they seek no wealth and encounter no trouble. Hence, they live long."

LI HSI-CHAI says, "If we love something, the more we love it, the more it costs us. If we treasure something, the more we treasure it, the more it exhausts us. A little of either results in shame. A lot results in ruin. And regret comes too late. People who are wise are not like this. They know that they have everything they need within themselves. Hence, they do not seek anything outside themselves. Thus, those who would shame them find nothing to shame. They know their own limit, and their limit is the Tao. Hence, they don't act unless it is according to the Tao. Thus, those who would trouble them find nothing to trouble. Hence, they survive and, surviving, live long."

HO-SHANG KUNG says, "Excessive sensual desire exhausts our spirit. Excessive material desire brings us misfortune. The living keep their treasures in storerooms. The dead keep their treasures in graves. The living worry about thieves. The dead worry about grave robbers. Those who know contentment find happiness and wealth within themselves and don't exhaust their spirit. If they should govern a country, they don't trouble their people. Thus, they are able to live long."

HUAI-NAN-TZU says, "Long ago Chih Po-ch'iao attacked and defeated Fan Chung-hsing. He also attacked the leaders of the states of Han and Wei and occupied parts of their territories. Still, he felt this wasn't enough, so he raised another army and attacked the state of Yueh. But Han and Wei counterattacked, and Chih's army was defeated near Chinyang, and he was killed east of Kaoliang. His skull became a drinking bowl, his kingdom was divided among the victors, and he was ridiculed by the world. This is what happens when you don't know when to stop" (*Huainantzu*: 18).

I have followed the Kuotien and Mawangtui A texts in prefacing line eleven with *ku* (therefore).

45

大成若缺。其用不弊。

大盈若沖。其用不窮。

大直若屈。大巧若拙。

大贏若絀。燥勝寒。静勝熱。

知清静。可以為天下正。

Perfectly complete it seems deficient
yet it never wears out
perfectly full it seems empty
yet it never runs dry
perfectly straight it seems crooked
perfectly clever it seems clumsy
perfectly abundant it seems impoverished
active it overcomes cold
still it overcomes heat
those who know how to be perfectly still
are able to govern the world

WU CH'ENG says, "To treat the complete as complete, the full as full, the straight as straight, and the clever as clever is mundane. To treat what seems deficient as complete, what seems empty as full, what seems crooked as straight, and what seems clumsy as clever, this is transcendent. This is the meaning of Lao-tzu's entire book: opposites complement each other."

LU NUNG-SHIH says, "What is most complete cannot be seen in its entirety, hence it seems deficient. What is fullest cannot be seen it its totality, hence it seems empty. What is straightest cannot be seen in its perfection, hence it seems crooked. What is cleverest cannot be seen in its brilliance, hence it seems clumsy."

SU CH'E says, "The world considers what is not deficient as complete, hence complete includes worn out. It considers what is not empty as full, hence full includes exhausted. The wise, however, do not mind if what is most complete is deficient or what is fullest is empty. For what is most complete never wears out, and what is fullest never runs dry."

HAN FEI says, "Ordinary people employ their spirit in activity. But activity means extravagance, and extravagance means wastefulness. Those who are wise employ their spirit in stillness. Stillness means moderation, and moderation means frugality."

SUNG CH'ANG-HSING says, "We keep warm in winter by moving around. But sooner or later, we stop moving and become cold again. We keep cool in summer by sitting still. But sooner or later, we stop sitting still and become hot again. This is not the way of long life. This is how what is complete becomes deficient, what is full becomes empty, what is straight becomes crooked, and what is clever becomes clumsy. Those who seek balance should look for it in perfect stillness. Perfect stillness is the essence of the Tao. Those who achieve such balance are free from hot and cold."

LI HSI-CHAI says, "Activity overcomes cold but cannot overcome heat. Stillness overcomes heat but cannot overcome cold. Perfect stillness or effortlessness doesn't try to overcome anything, yet nothing in the world can overcome it. Thus is it said that perfect stillness can govern the world."

CONFUCIUS says, "Those who govern with virtue are like the North Star, which remains in its place, while the myriad stars revolve around it" (*Lunyu*: 2.1).

In the Wangpi and Fuyi editions, line seven reads: "what is most eloquent seems dumb." I have replaced this with the version introduced by Mawangtui B, with which the commentary of Yen Tsun agrees, and with which the Kuotien texts also seem to agree (reading *ch'eng* [success] as graphic shorthand for *sheng* [abundant]). Some commentators have wondered if lines eight and nine are not corrupt. Some, for example, have suggested "cold it overcomes heat / still it overcomes activity" would be more in keeping with Lao-tzu's usage of these terms in verse 26. However, there is no support for such a variant among early texts, and I have accepted both lines as they stand. In line ten, I have gone along with the Fuyi text's addition of *chih* (know how). And in the last line, I have followed Mawangtui A in adding *k'o* (able). Also in the last line, the Kuotien edition has *ting* (pacify) in place of *cheng* (govern), but no other text has this variant.

46

天下有道。
卻走馬以糞。
天下無道。
戎馬生於郊。
罪莫大於可欲。
禍莫大於不知足。
咎莫憯於欲得。
故知足之足。
恆足矣。

When the Tao is present in the world
courier horses manure fields instead of roads
when the Tao is absent from the world
war horses are raised on the border
no crime is worse than yielding to desire
no wrong is greater than discontent
no curse is crueler than getting what you want
the contentment of being content
is true contentment indeed

HO-SHANG KUNG says, "'When the Tao is present' means when the world's rulers possess the Tao. In ordering their countries, they don't use weapons, and they send courier horses back to do farm work. And in ordering themselves, they redirect their *yang* essence to fertilize their bodies."

YEN TSUN says, "The lives of the people depend on their ruler. And the position of the ruler depends on the people. When a ruler possesses the Tao, the people prosper. When a ruler loses the Tao, the people suffer."

WANG PI says, "When the Tao is present, contentment reigns. People don't seek external things but cultivate themselves instead. Courier horses are sent home to manure fields. When people don't control their desires, when they don't cultivate themselves but seek external things instead, cavalry horses are bred on the borders."

WU CH'ENG says, "In ancient times, every district of sixty-four neighborhoods was required to provide a horse for the army."

CHIAO HUNG says, "A 'border' refers to the land between two states. When war horses are raised on the border, it means soldiers have not been home for a long time."

THE *YENTIEHLUN* says, "It is said that long ago, before the wars with the Northern Hu and the Southern Yueh, taxes were low, and the people were well off. Their clothes were warm, and their larders were stocked. Cattle and horses grazed in herds. Farmers used horses to pull plows and carts. Nobody rode them. During this period, even the swiftest horses were used to manure fields. Later, when armies arose, there were never enough horses for the cavalry, and mares were used as well. Thus, colts were born on the battlefield" (15).

LI HSI-CHAI says, "When the ruler possesses the Tao, soldiers become farmers. When the ruler does not possess the Tao, farmers become soldiers. Someone who understands the Tao turns form into emptiness. Someone who does not understand the Tao turns emptiness into form. To yield to desire means to want. Not to know contentment means to grasp. To get what you want means to possess. Want gives birth to grasping, and grasping gives birth to possessing, and there is no end to possessing. But once we know that we do not need to grasp anything outside ourselves, we know contentment. And once we know contentment, there is nothing with which we are not content."

LU HSI-SHENG says, "When the mind sees something desirable and wants it, even though it does not accord with reason — there is no worse crime. When want knows no limit, and it brings harm to others, there is no greater wrong. When every desire has to be satisfied, and the mind never stops burning, there is no crueler curse. We all have enough. When we are content with enough, we are content wherever we are."

LU TUNG-PIN says, "To know contentment means the Tao prevails. Not to know contentment means the Tao fails. What we know comes from our minds, which Lao-tzu represents as a horse. When we know contentment, our horse stays home. When we don't know contentment, it guards the border. When the Tao prevails, we put the whip away."

HSUAN-TSUNG says, "Material contentment is not contentment. Spiritual contentment is true contentment."

The Kuotien texts omit the first four lines and reverse the order of lines five and six, while the Wangpi edition omits line five.

47

不見而名。不為而成。
是以聖人不行而知。
其出彌遠。其知彌少。
不窺於牖。以知天道。
不出於戶。以知天下。

Without going out your door
you can know the whole world
without looking out your window
you can know the Way of Heaven
the farther people go
the less they know
sages therefore know without traveling
name without seeing
and succeed without trying

CHUANG-TZU says, "Who takes Heaven as their ancestor, Virtue as their home, the Tao as their door, and who escapes change is a sage" (*Chuangtzu*: 33.1).

HO-SHANG KUNG says, "Those who are sages understand other individuals by understanding themselves. They understand other families by understanding their own family. Thus, they understand the whole world. Humankind and Heaven are linked to each other. If the ruler is content, the breath of Heaven will be calm. If the ruler is greedy, Heaven's breath will be unstable. Sages do not have to ascend into the sky or descend into the depths to understand Heaven or Earth."

WANG PI says, "Events have a beginning. Creatures have a leader. Roads diverge, but they lead back together. Thoughts multiply, but they all share one thing. The Way has one constant. Reason has one principle. Holding on to the ancient Way, we are able to master the present. Although we live today, we can understand the distant past. We can understand without going outside. If we don't understand, going farther only leads us farther astray."

SU CH'E says, "The reason the sages of the past understood everything without going anywhere was simply because they kept their natures whole. People let themselves be misled by things and allow their natures to be split into ears and eyes, body and mind. Their vision becomes limited to sights, and their hearing becomes limited to sounds."

WANG P'ANG says, "If we wait to see before we become aware and wait to become aware before we know, we can see ten thousand different views and still be blind to the reason that binds them all together."

LI HSI-CHAI says, "Those who look for Heaven and Earth outside look for forms. But Heaven and Earth cannot be fathomed through form, only through reason. Once we realize that reason is right here, it doesn't matter if we close our door. For those who are wise, knowledge is not limited to form. Hence, they don't have to go anywhere. Name is not limited to matter. Hence, they don't have to look anywhere. Success is not limited to action. Hence, they don't have to do anything."

LAO-TZU says, "The name that becomes a name / is not the Immortal Name" (*Taoteching*: 1).

CH'ENG HSUAN-YING says, "'Without traveling' means to know without depending on previous or external experience. 'Without seeing' means to know that everything is empty and that there is nothing to see. 'Without trying' means to focus the spirit on the tranquillity that excels at making things happen."

WU CH'ENG says, "'To succeed without trying' is the result of the previous two lines. Because those sages know everything without going anywhere and see everything without looking at anything, they succeed at everything without any effort at all."

Some commentators wonder if line eight is not corrupt, if *ming* (name) is not a mistake for *ming* (understand), and if the line should not then read: "understand without seeing." However, the only early edition that supports such an emendation is that of Han Fei. In a similar sequence, the *Chungyung*: 26.6 has: "flourish without displaying / change without moving / and succeed without trying."

48

為學者日益。為道者日損。
損之又損之。以至於無為。
無為則無不為。
及其有事。不足以取天下。
取天下恆無事。

Those who seek learning gain every day
those who seek the Way lose every day
they lose and they lose
until they find nothing to do
nothing to do means nothing not done
those who rule the world aren't busy
those who are busy
can't rule the world

HO-SHANG KUNG says, "'Learning' refers to knowledge of administration and rhetoric, ritual and music."

CONFUCIUS asked Tzu-kung, "Do you think I learn in order to increase my knowledge?" Tzu-kung answered, "Well, don't you?" Confucius replied, "No. I seek the one thing that ties everything together" (*Lunyu*: 15.2).

SUNG CH'ANG-HSING says, "Those who seek the Tao don't use their ears or eyes. They look within, not without. They obey their natures, not their desires. They don't value knowledge. They consider gaining as losing and losing as gaining."

YEN TSUN says, "Get rid of knowledge. The knowledge of no knowledge is the ancestor of all knowledge and the teacher of Heaven and Earth."

WANG PI says, "Those who seek learning seek to improve their ability or to increase their mastery, while those who seek the Tao seek to return to emptiness and nothingness. When something is done, something is left out. When nothing is done, nothing is not done."

HUAI-NAN-TZU says, "Those who are wise cultivate the inner root and do not make a display of the outer twigs. They protect their spirit and eliminate cleverness. They do nothing, which means they don't act until others act. And yet there is nothing that isn't done, which means they rely on the actions of others" (*Huainantzu*: 1).

TE-CH'ING says, "Those who seek the Tao begin by using wisdom to eliminate desires. Thus, they lose. Once their desires are gone, they eliminate wisdom. Thus, they lose again. And they go on like this until the mind and the world are both forgotten, until selfish desires are completely eliminated, until they reach the state of doing nothing. And while they do nothing, the people transform themselves. Thus, by doing nothing, the sage can do great things. Hence, those who would rule the world should know the value of not being busy."

KUMARAJIVA says, "Those who lose eliminate everything coarse until they forget about the bad. Then they eliminate everything fine until they forget about the good. The bad is what they dislike. The good is what they like. First, they eliminate dislikes. Then, they eliminate likes. Once they forget their likes and dislikes and cut themselves off from desire, their virtue becomes one with the Tao, and they reach the state of doing nothing. And while they do nothing, they let others do what they want. Hence, there is nothing that isn't done."

SU CH'E says, "Everyone wants to rule the world. But when people see others doing something to possess it, they cringe. And when the people see the sage doing nothing, they rejoice. Those who are wise do not seek to rule the world. The world comes to them."

TS'AO TAO-CH'UNG says, "When someone uses laws to restrict the world, might to compel it, knowledge to silence it, and majesty to impress it, there are always those who don't follow. When someone rules by means of the Tao, the world follows without thinking. 'The world' refers to the ten thousand things."

WEN-TZU says, "In ancient times, those who were good rulers imitated the sea. The sea becomes great by doing nothing. Doing nothing, it governs hundreds of rivers and streams. Thus, it rules by not being busy" (*Wentzu*: 8).

Although the Kuotien texts omit the last three lines, they are present in all other editions and are present or implied (by the spaces) in both Mawangtui texts.

49

聖人恆無心。以
百姓之心為心。善者吾善之。
不善者吾亦善之。得善矣。信者吾信之。
不信者吾亦信之。得信矣。
聖人之在天下歙歙焉。為天下渾其心。
百姓皆注其耳目。聖人皆閡之。

Sages have no mind of their own
their mind is the mind of the people
to the good they are good
to the bad they are good
until they become good
to the true they are true
to the false they are true
until they become true
in the world sages are withdrawn
with the world they merge their mind
people open their ears and eyes
sages cover theirs up

SU CH'E says, "Emptiness has no form. It takes on the form of the ten thousand things. If emptiness had its own form it could not form anything else. Thus, sages have no mind of their own. They take on the minds of the people and treat everyone the same."

HUI-TSUNG says, "Because it is empty, the mind of a sage can receive. Because it is still, it can respond."

YEN TSUN says, "A mindless mind is the chief of all minds. Sages, therefore, have no mind of their own but embrace the minds of the people. Free of love and hate, they are not the enemy of evil or the friend of the good. They are not the protector of truth or the adversary of falsehood. They support like the earth and cover like the sky. They illuminate like the sun and transform like the spirit."

WANG P'ANG says, "Good and bad are the result of delusions, and delusions are the result of self-centered minds. Those who open themselves up to the Great Way, although their eyes see good and bad, their minds do not distinguish any differences. They don't treat the bad with goodness out of pity but because they don't perceive any difference. Although the ten thousand things are different, their differences are equally real and equally false. To see the real in the false and the false in the real is how the wisdom of sages differs from that of others."

CONFUCIUS says, "In their dealings with the world, great people are neither for nor against anyone. They follow whatever is right" (*Lunyu*: 4.10).

WANG PI says, "The mind of sages has no point of view, and their thoughts have no direction."

JEN FA-JUNG says, "Wherever sages go in the world, they act humble and withdrawn and blend in with others. They treat everyone, noble or commoner, rich or poor, with the same kindness and equality. Their mind merges with that of others. Ordinary people concentrate on what they hear and see and concern themselves with their own welfare. The sage's mind is like that of a newborn baby, pure and impartial."

HSUAN-TSUNG says, "Sages cover up the tracks of their mind by blending in with others."

CH'ENG HSUAN-YING says, "Stop the eyes and the ears, and the other senses will follow."

The Chinese word for mind, *hsin*, also means "thoughts," "goals," "intentions," or "will." Thus, Lao-tzu is not being philosophical here in saying "sages have no mind of their own," merely practical. In lines five and eight, some editions have *te* (virtue) in place of *te* (until). Although the two characters were interchangeable, I have sided with the Fuyi and Yentsun editions in choosing "until." For lines eleven and twelve, most commentators read: "the people focus their ears and eyes on the sages / and the sages treat them like babies." But in verses 10, 20, 28, and 55, Lao-tzu likens the sage, not the people, to a child. I suspect the text is corrupt here. Unfortunately, both Mawangtui texts are indecipherable, and the Kuotien texts do not include this verse. Meanwhile the Fuyi variation of *k'o* (cough), the Tunhuang variation of *hai* (suffer), and the Yentsun variation of *hai* (startle) are clearly loans. But loans for what? Most commentators argue for *hai* (infant). I've gone along with Kao Heng, who suggests *ai* (obstruct).

50

兵無所容其刃。夫何故。以其無死地。

陵行不遇兕虎。兕無所投其角。虎無所措其爪。

以其生生。蓋聞善攝生者。入軍不被甲兵。

而民生生。動皆之死地之十有三。夫何故。

出生。入死。生之徒十有三。死之徒十有三。

Appearing means life
disappearing means death
thirteen are the followers of life
thirteen are the followers of death
but people living to live
move toward the land of death's thirteen
and why is this so
because they live to live
it's said that those who guard life well
aren't injured by soldiers in battle
or harmed by rhinos or tigers in the wild
for rhinos find nowhere to stick their horns
tigers find nowhere to sink their claws
and soldiers find nowhere to thrust their spears
and why is this so
because for them there's no land of death

CH'ENG CHU says, "Of the ten thousand changes we all experience, none are more important than life and death. People who cultivate the Tao are concerned with nothing except transcending these boundaries."

In lines three, four and six, the phrase *shih-yu-san* has long puzzled commentators. HAN FEI says it means "three and ten," or thirteen, and refers to the four limbs and nine orifices of the body, which can be guarded to preserve life or indulged to end it.

TU ER-WEI says the numerical significance of thirteen here refers to the moon, which becomes full thirteen days after it first appears and which disappears thirteen days after it begins to wane.

WANG PI says it means "three in ten" and refers to the three basic attitudes people have toward life. Wang An-shih summarizes these as: "Among ten people, three seek life because they hate death, three seek death because they hate life, and three live as if they were dead." Leaving the sage, who neither hates death nor loves life, but who thus lives long.

The Mawangtui texts, which I have followed here, word lines five and six in such a way as to make Wang Pi's interpretation unlikely, if not impossible. As for choosing between Han Fei and Tu Er-wei, I think Professor Tu's interpretation comes closer to what Lao-tzu had in mind.

WANG PI also says, "Eels consider the depths too shallow, and eagles consider the mountains too low. Living beyond the reach of arrows and nets, they both dwell in the land of no death. But by means of baits, they are lured into the land of no life."

SU CH'E says, "We know how to act but not how to rest. We know how to talk but not how to keep quiet. We know how to remember but not how to forget. Everything we do leads to the land of death. The sage dwells where there is neither life nor death."

TE-CH'ING says, "Those who guard their life don't cultivate life but what controls life. What has life is form. What controls life is nature. When we cultivate our nature, we return to what is real and forget bodily form. Once we forget form, our self becomes empty. Once our self is empty, nothing can harm us. Once there is no self, there is no life. How then could there be any death?"

CHIAO HUNG says, "Those who are wise have no life. Not because they slight it, but because they don't possess it. If someone has no life, how can they be killed? Those who understand this can transcend change and make of life and death a game."

I have followed the Mawangtui wording of lines five, six, and eight. Some editions add the last two lines to verse 75. This verse is not present in the Kuotien texts.

51

生而不有。為而不恃。長而不宰。是謂玄德。
而貴德。道之尊。德之貴。夫莫之爵。而恆自然。
道生之畜之。長之育之。亭之毒之。養之覆之。
道生之。德畜之。物形之。器成之。是以萬物尊道。

The Way begets them
Virtue keeps them
matter shapes them
usage completes them
thus do all creatures respect the Way
and honor Virtue
their respect for the Way
and honor of Virtue
are not conferred
but simply natural
for the Way begets and keeps them
raises and trains them
steadies and adjusts them
maintains and protects them
but it doesn't possess what it begets
or depend on what it develops
or control what it raises
this is called Dark Virtue

WU CH'ENG says, "What is begotten is sprouted in spring; what is kept is collected in fall; what is shaped is raised in summer from sprouts grown in spring; what is completed is stored in winter from the harvest of fall. Sprouting, raising, harvesting, and storing all depend on the Way and Virtue. Hence, the ten thousand creatures respect the Tao as their father and honor Virtue as their mother. The Way and Virtue are two, but also one. In spring, from one root many are begotten: the Way becomes Virtue. In fall, the many are brought back together: Virtue becomes the Way. The Way and Virtue are mentioned at the beginning of this verse, but only the Way is mentioned later [in line eleven]. This is because Virtue is also the Way."

LI HSI-CHAI says, "What the Way and Virtue bestow, they bestow without thought. No one orders them. It is simply their nature. It is their nature to beget and their nature to keep. It is their nature to raise and train, to steady and adjust, to maintain and protect. And because it's their nature, they never tire of begetting or expect a reward for what they give. This is what is meant by 'Dark Virtue.'"

LU HSI-SHENG says, "To beget is to endow with essence. To keep is to instill with breath. To raise is to adapt to form. To train is to bring forth ability. To steady is to weigh the end. To adjust is to measure the use. To maintain is to preserve the balance. To protect is to keep from harm. This is the Great Way. It begets but does not try to possess what it begets. It develops but does not depend on what it develops. It raises but does not try to control what it raises. This is Dark Virtue. In verse 10, Humankind is likened to the Way and Virtue. Here, the Way and Virtue are likened to Humankind. The expressions are the same, and so is the meaning."

HO-SHANG KUNG says, "The Way does not beget the myriad creatures to possess them for its own advantage. The actions of the Way do not depend on a reward. And the Way does not raise or maintain the myriad creatures to butcher them for profit. The kindness performed by the Way is dark and invisible." Where Ho-shang Kung reads "butcher," Lu Hsi-sheng reads "control." I have followed Lu.

WANG PI says, "The Way is what things follow. Virtue is what they attain. 'Dark Virtue' means virtue is present but no one knows who controls it. It comes from what is hidden."

In line four, I have followed the Mawangtui texts in reading *ch'i* (usage) for *shih* (condition). I have also gone along with the Mawangtui texts in omitting *mo-pu* (none does not) from line five and have used their version of line thirteen, in which *ting* (steady) and *tu* (adjust) appear in place of *ch'eng* (mature) and *shu* (ripen).

52

終身不勤。開其兌。濟其事。終身不救。見小曰明。
既知其子。復守其母。沒身不殆。塞其兌。閉其門。
天下有始。以為天下母。既得其母。以知其子。
守柔曰強。用其光。復歸其明。無遺身殃。是謂襲常。

There's a maiden in the world
who becomes the world's mother
those who find the mother
thereby know the child
those who know the child
keep the mother safe
and live without trouble
those who block the opening
who close the gate
live without toil
those who unblock the opening
who meddle in affairs
live without hope
those who see the small have vision
those who protect the weak have strength
those who use their light
and trust their vision
live beyond death
this is called holding on to the crescent

LAO-TZU says, "The maiden of Heaven and Earth has no name / the mother of all things has a name" (*Taoteching:* 1).

KUAN-TZU says, "The ancients say, 'No one understands a child better than its father. No one understands a minister better than his ruler'" (*Kuantzu:* 7).

LI HSI-CHAI says, "The Way is the mother of all creatures. All creatures are the children of the Way. In ancient times, those who possessed the Way were able to keep mother and children from parting and the Way and all creatures together. Since creatures come from the Way, they are no different from the Way, just as children are no different from their mother. And yet people abandon other creatures when they search for the Way. Is this any different from abandoning the children while searching for the mother? If people knew that all creatures are the Way, and children are the mother, they would find the source in everything they meet."

CONFUCIUS says, "Things have their roots and branches. Those who know what comes first and last approach the Tao" (*Tahsueh*).

TUNG SSU-CHING says, "People are born when they receive breath. Breath is their mother. And spirit dwells within their breath. When children care for their mother, their breath becomes one and their spirit becomes still."

WU CH'ENG says, "'Opening' refers to the mouth. 'Gate' refers to the nose. By controlling our breath to the point where there is no breath, where breath is concentrated within, we are never exhausted."

WANG P'ANG says, "When the opening opens, things enter. And the spirit is exhausted trying to deal with the problems that then develop. Once we are swept away by this flood, who can save us?"

HSUAN-TSUNG says, "Those who can see an event while it is still small and change their behavior accordingly we say have vision."

WANG PI says, "Seeing what is great is not vision. Seeing what is small is vision. Protecting the strong is not strength. Protecting the weak is strength."

WANG AN-SHIH says, "Light is the function of vision. Vision is the embodiment of light. If we can use the light to find our way back to the source, we can live our lives free of misfortune and become one with the Immortal Way."

This verse reminds me of Confucius' words: "When I was young, historians still left blanks" (*Lunyu*: 15.25). Not being a historian, I have proceeded despite uncertainty. In the last line, the word *hsi* means "to wear" but also "to hold on to." And the word *ch'ang* normally means "constant," but it is the name of the crescent moon as well.

53

使我介有知。行於大道。唯迤是畏。
大道甚夷。而民好徑。朝甚除。田甚蕪。
倉甚虛。服文采。帶利劍。厭飲食。
貨財有餘。是謂盜夸。盜夸非道哉。

Were I sufficiently wise
I would follow the Great Way
and only fear going astray
the Great Way is smooth
but people love byways
their palaces are spotless
but their fields are overgrown
and their granaries are empty
they wear fine clothes
and carry sharp swords
they tire of food and drink
and possess more than they need
this is called robbery
and robbery is not the Way

KU HSI-CH'OU says, "The Tao is not hard to know, but it is hard to follow."

HO-SHANG KUNG says, "Lao-tzu was concerned that rulers of his day did not follow the Great Way. Hence, he hypothesized that if he knew enough to conduct the affairs of a country, he would follow the Great Way and devote himself to implementing the policy of doing nothing."

LU HSI-SHENG says, "The Great Way is like a grand thoroughfare: smooth and easy to travel, perfectly straight and free of detours, and there is nowhere it doesn't lead. But people are in a hurry. They take shortcuts and get into trouble and become lost and don't reach their destination. The sage worries only about leading people down such a path."

LI HSI-CHAI says, "A spotless palace refers to the height of superficiality. An overgrown field refers to an uncultivated mind. An empty granary refers to a lack of virtue."

HAN FEI says, "When the court is in good repair, lawsuits abound. When lawsuits abound, fields become overgrown. When fields become overgrown, granaries become empty. When granaries become empty, the country becomes poor. When the country becomes poor, customs become decadent, and there is no trick people don't try" (*Hanfeitzu*: 20).

SUNG CH'ANG HSING says, "When the court ignores the affairs of state to beautify its halls and interrupts farm work to build towers and pavilions, the people's energy ends up at court, and fields turn to weeds. Once fields turn to weeds, state taxes are not paid and granaries become empty. And once granaries are empty, the country becomes poor, and the people become rebellious. The court dazzles the people with its fine clothes, and threatens the people with its sharp swords, and takes from people more than it needs—this is no different from robbing them."

LI JUNG says, "A robber is someone who never has enough and who takes more than he needs."

WANG PI says, "To gain possession of something by means other than the Way is wrong. And wrong means robbery."

Wang Nien-sun sees a problem with the standard version of line three, which reads: "only fear acting." Wang suggests *shih* (act) is a mistake for *yi* (go astray), and I agree. This verse is absent in the Kuotien texts, but both Mawangtui texts have *t'a* (he), which is clearly a mistake, but it makes *yi* just as likely as *shih*. The three characters are nearly identical. In the last two lines, *tao* (rob) is followed by *k'ua* (grand) in the Fuyi edition and by the absence of text in the Mawangtui editions. I have read *k'ua* as a mistake for a nearly identical character, *hsi*, which functions like a comma and which provides a sharper delineation of the pun at work here. The words for robbery and Way are both pronounced *tao*.

54

善建者不拔。善抱者不脫。子孫以祭祀不絕。
修之身其德乃真。修之家其德乃餘。修之鄉其德乃長。
修之邦其德乃豐。修之天下其德乃博。
故以身觀身。以家觀家。以鄉觀鄉。以邦觀邦。
以天下觀天下。吾何以知天下之然。以此。

What you plant well can't be uprooted
what you hold well can't be taken away
your descendents will worship this forever
cultivated in yourself virtue becomes real
cultivated in your family virtue grows
cultivated in your village virtue multiplies
cultivated in your state virtue abounds
cultivated in your world virtue is everywhere
thus view others through yourself
view families through your family
view villages through your village
view states through your state
view other worlds through your world
how do you know what other worlds are like
through this one

WU CH'ENG says, "Those who plant something well, plant it without planting. Thus, it is never uprooted. Those who hold something well, hold it without holding. Thus, it is never taken away."

WANG AN-SHIH says, "What we plant well is virtue. What we hold well is oneness. When virtue flourishes, distant generations give praise."

TS'AO TAO-CH'UNG says, "First improve yourself, then reach out to others and to later generations bequeath the noble, pure, and kindly Tao. Thus, blessings reach your descendants, virtue grows, beauty lasts, and worship never ends."

SUNG CH'ANG-HSING says, "In ancient times, ancestral worship consisted in choosing an auspicious day before the full moon, in fasting, in selecting sacrificial animals, in purifying the ritual vessels, in preparing a feast on the appointed day, in venerating ancestors as if they were present, and in thanking them for their virtuous example. Those who cultivate the Way likewise enable later generations to enjoy the fruits of their cultivation."

HO-SHANG KUNG says, "We cultivate the Tao in ourselves by cherishing our breath and by nourishing our spirit and thus by prolonging our life. We cultivate the Tao in our family by being loving as a parent, filial as a child, kind as an elder, obedient as the younger, dependable as a husband, and chaste as a wife. We cultivate the Tao in our village by honoring the aged and caring for the young, by teaching the benighted and instructing the perverse. We cultivate the Tao in our state by being honest as an official and loyal as an aide. We cultivate the Tao in the world by letting things change without giving orders. Lao-tzu asks how we know that those who cultivate the Tao prosper and those who ignore the Tao perish. We know by comparing those who don't cultivate the Tao with those who do."

YEN TSUN says, "Let your person be the yardstick of other persons. Let your family be the level of other families. Let your village be the square of other villages. Let your state be the plumb line of other states. As for the world, the ruler is its heart, and the world is his body."

CHUANG-TZU says, "The reality of the Tao lies in concern for the self. Concern for the state is irrelevant, and concern for the world is cowshit. From this standpoint, the emperor's work is the sage's hobby and is not what develops the self or nourishes life" (*Chuangtzu*: 28.3).

The same sentiments were echoed by Confucius in the *Tahsueh* (Great Learning): "The ancients who wished to manifest Virtue in the world first ordered their states. Wishing to order their states, they first harmonized their families. Wishing to harmonize their families, they first cultivated themselves. Wishing to cultivate themselves, they first perfected their minds. Wishing to perfect their minds, they first rectified their thoughts. Wishing to rectify their thoughts, they first deepened their knowledge" (4). As in verse 36, Mawangtui A has *pang* (state), while Mawangtui B has the synonym *kuo* (country), suggesting A was copied before 206 B.C., when the use of *pang* was forbidden, as it was part of the emperor's name. In line nine, both Mawangtui texts omit *ku* (thus), while the Fuyi and Wangpi editions include it. The Kuotien texts omit line nine. The meaning of the last seven lines is similar to that of the line in the poem "Carving an Ax Handle" in the *Book of Songs:* "In carving an ax handle, the pattern is not far off."

55

含德之厚者。比於赤子。蜂蠆不螫。猛獸不攫。
鷙鳥不搏。骨弱筋柔。而握固。未知牝牡之合。
而朘作。精之至。終日號。而不嗄。和之至。
知和曰常。知常曰明。益生曰祥。心使氣曰強。
物壯則老。謂之不道。不道早已。

He who possesses virtue in abundance
resembles a newborn child
wasps don't sting him
beasts don't claw him
birds of prey don't carry him off
his bones are weak and his tendons soft
yet his grip is firm
he hasn't known the union of sexes
yet his penis is stiff
so full of essence is he
he cries all day
yet never gets hoarse
his breath is so perfectly balanced
knowing how to be balanced we endure
knowing how to endure we become wise
while those who lengthen their life tempt luck
and those who force their breath become strong
but once things mature they become old
this isn't the Way
what isn't the Way ends early

WANG P'ANG says, "The nature of Virtue is lasting abundance. But its abundance fades with the onset of thoughts and desires."

SU CH'E says, "Once we have a mind, we have a body. And once we have a body, we have enemies. If we did not have a mind, we would not have enemies and could not be harmed. The reason a newborn child isn't harmed is because it has no mind."

HO-SHANG KUNG says, "A newborn child doesn't harm anyone, and no one harms it. In an age of perfect peace, Humankind knows neither noble nor base. Even wild beasts do people no harm."

TE-CH'ING says, "Those who cultivate the Tao should first focus their mind. When their mind doesn't stray, they become calm. When their mind becomes calm, their breath becomes balanced. When their breath becomes balanced, their essence becomes stable, their spirit becomes serene, and their true nature is restored. Once we know how to breathe, we know how to endure. And once we know how to endure, we know our true nature. If we don't know our true nature but only know how to nourish our body and lengthen our life, we end up harming our body and destroying our life. A restless mind disturbs the breath. When our breath is disturbed, our essence weakens. And when our essence weakens, our body withers."

HSUN-TZU says, "Everything must breathe to live. When we know how to breathe, we know how to nurture life and how to endure" (*Hsuntzu:* 17).

SUNG CH'ANG-HSING says, "The basis of life rests on this breath. If people can nourish the pure and balanced breath within themselves for fifteen minutes, they will discover the principle of Heaven and Earth's immortality. If they can do this for half an hour, they will enter the gate of eternity. But if they try to extend their life or force their breath, they will create the womb of their own destruction."

WANG AN-SHIH says, "Life cannot be extended. But people keep trying and thus incur misfortune."

MOU-TZU says, "Those who attain the Way don't become active and don't become strong. They don't become strong and don't become old. They don't become old and don't become ill. They don't become ill and don't decay. Thus, Lao-tzu calls the body a disaster" (*Moutzu:* 32).

Scientists talk about the Big Bang. No one talks about the Big Breath. The Mawang-tui and Kuotien texts compress lines three through five into two lines. In lines thirteen and fourteen, I have followed *Huainantzu:* 2 and the *Huangti Neiching:* 69–70 in reading *ho* (gentle/balanced) as short for *ho-ch'i* (gentle/balanced breath). Neither the Mawangtui texts nor the Kuotien texts have *chih* (to know how) at the beginning of line fourteen. But all later editions do, and without it, the line itself is unbalanced. Line fifteen also appears in verse 16, and the last three lines also occur at the end of verse 30 (although my translation of them varies). The Kuotien texts omit the last line.

56

不可得而貴。亦不可得而賤。故為天下貴。
不可得而利。亦不可得而害。
不可得而親。亦不可得而疏。
挫其銳。解其紛。和其光。同其塵。是謂玄同。
知者不言。言者不知。塞其兌。閉其門。

Those who know don't talk

those who talk don't know

seal the opening

close the gate

dull the edge

untie the tangle

soften the light

and join the dust

this is called the Dark Union

it can't be embraced

it can't be abandoned

it can't be helped

it can't be harmed

it can't be exalted

it can't be debased

thus does the world exalt it

HO-SHANG KUNG says, "Those who know, value deeds not words. A team of horses can't overtake the tongue. More talk means more problems."

TS'AO TAO-CH'UNG says, "Those who grasp the truth forget about words. Those who don't practice what they talk about are no different from those who don't know."

SU CH'E says, "The Tao isn't talk, but it doesn't exclude talk. Those who know don't necessarily talk. Those who talk don't necessarily know."

HUANG YUAN-CHI says, "We seal the opening and close the gate to nourish the breath. We dull the edge and untie the tangle to still the spirit. We soften the light and join the dust to adapt to the times and get along with the world."

LI HSI-CHAI says, "By sealing the opening, we guard the exit. By closing the gate, we bar the entrance. By dulling the edge, we adjust the inside. By untying the tangle, we straighten the outside. By softening the light, we focus on ourselves. By joining the dust, we adapt to others. What is devoid of exit and entrance, inside and outside, self and other, we call the Dark Union."

WANG TAO says, "The Dark Union unites all things but leaves no visible trace."

WANG PI says, "If something can be embraced, it can be abandoned. If something can be helped, it can be harmed. If something can be exalted, it can be debased."

TE-CH'ING says, "Those who know transcend the mundane and the superficial, hence they cannot be embraced. Their utter honesty enables others to see. Hence, they cannot be abandoned. They are content and free of desires. Hence, they cannot be helped. They dwell beyond life and death. Hence, they cannot be harmed. They view high position as so much dust. Hence, they cannot be exalted. Beneath their rags they harbor jade. Hence, they cannot be debased. Those who know walk in the world, yet their minds transcend the material realm. Hence, they are exalted by the world."

WEI YUAN says, "Those who seal the opening and close the gate neither love nor hate. Hence, they don't embrace or abandon anything. Those who dull the edge and untie the tangle don't seek help. Thus, they suffer no harm. Those who soften the light and join the dust don't exalt themselves. Thus, they aren't debased by others. Forgetting self and other, they experience Dark Union with the Tao. Those who have not yet experienced this Dark Union unite with 'this' and separate from 'that.' To unite means to embrace, to help, and to exalt. To separate means to abandon, to harm, and to debase. Those who experience Dark Union unite with nothing. From what, then, could they separate?"

Knowing comes before talking. And the Dark Union comes before knowing. It's called the Dark Union because it precedes the division into subject and object. The Kuotien texts insert *chih* (it) in lines one and two, resulting in a reading of "Those who know it don't talk about it / those who talk about it don't know it." Lines three and four also occur in verse 52, and lines five through eight appear in verse 4 (although my translation of them there is different). The Kuotien and Mawangtui texts have a slightly different order for lines three through eight, and they begin line ten with *ku* (thus).

57

以正治邦。以奇用兵。以無事取天下。吾何以知其然哉。

夫天下多忌諱。而民彌貧。民多利器。而邦家滋昏。

民多智巧。而奇物滋起。法物滋彰。而盜賊多有。

是以聖人之言曰。我無事。而民自化。我好靜。

而民自正。我無事。而民自富。我無欲。而民自朴。

Use directness to govern a country

and use deception to fight a war

but use nonaction to rule the world

how do we know this works

the greater the prohibitions

the poorer the people

the sharper their tools

the more chaotic the realm

the cleverer their schemes

the more common the bizarre

the better their possessions

the more numerous the thieves

thus does the sage declare

I make no effort

and the people transform themselves

I stay still

and the people correct themselves

I do no work

and the people enrich themselves

I want nothing

and the people simplify themselves

SUN-TZU says, "In waging war, one attacks with directness, one wins with deception" (*Suntzu Pingfa*: 5.5).

WANG AN-SHIH says, "Directness can be used in governing, but nowhere else. Deception can be used in warfare, but that is all. Only those who practice nonaction are fit to rule the world."

SU CH'E says, "The ancient sages were kind to strangers and gentle to friends. They didn't think about warfare. Only when they had no choice did they fight. And when they did, they used deception. But deception can't be used to rule the world. The world is a mercurial thing. To conquer it is to lose it. Those who embody the Tao do nothing. They don't rule the world, and yet the world comes to them."

LU HUI-CH'ING says, "How do we know we can rule the world by means of non-action? Because we know we cannot rule the world by means of action."

TE-CH'ING says, "Prohibitions, tools, schemes, possessions, all of these involve action and cannot be used to rule the world."

WANG PI says, "Prohibitions are intended to put an end to poverty, and yet the people become poorer. Tools are intended to strengthen the country, and yet the country becomes weaker and more chaotic. This is due to cultivating the branches instead of the roots."

WANG P'ANG says, "Prohibitions interfere with the people's livelihood. Thus, poverty increases. Sharp tools mean sharp minds. And sharp minds mean chaos and confusion. Once minds become refined, customs become depraved, and the monstrous becomes commonplace."

HO-SHANG KUNG says, "In cultivating the Tao, sages accept the will of Heaven. They don't change things, and the people transform themselves. They prefer not to talk or teach, and the people correct themselves. They don't force others to work, and the people become rich at their occupations. They don't use ornaments or luxuries, and the people emulate their simple ways."

CONFUCIUS says, "The virtue of the ruler is like wind. The virtue of the people is like grass. When the wind blows, the grass bends" (*Lunyu*: 12.19).

My mother used to say, "If wishes were horses, beggars would ride." At the end of line four, the Fuyi, the Suotan, and Wangpi editions answer with *yi-tz'u* (because of this). I have followed the Kuotien and Mawangtui texts, which omit this phrase. In line six, the Kuotien texts have "the more *rebellious* the people." But no other text follows suit. In most editions, line eleven has *fa-ling* (laws and orders). I have gone along with the Kuotien texts, Mawangtui B, and Ho-shang Kung, all of which have *fa-wu* (fine things).

58

其政悶悶。其民淳淳。其政察察。其民缺缺。
禍兮福之所倚。福兮禍之所伏。孰知其極。
其無正也。正復為奇。善復為妖。民之迷也。
其日固久矣。是以聖人方而不割。廉而不劌。直而不肆。光而不曜。

Where the government stands aloof
the people open up
where the government steps in
the people slip away
happiness rests in misery
misery hides in happiness
who knows where these end
for nothing is direct
directness becomes deception
and good becomes evil
the people have been lost
for a long long time
thus the sage is an edge that doesn't cut
a point that doesn't pierce
a line that doesn't extend
a light that doesn't blind

HSUAN-TSUNG says, "To stand aloof is to be relaxed and unconcerned. To open up is to be simple and honest. The ruler who governs without effort lets things take care of themselves."

WANG PI says, "Those who are good at governing use neither laws nor measures. Thus, the people find nothing to attack."

LI HSI-CHAI says, "When the government makes no demands, the people respond with openness instead of cleverness. When the government makes demands, the people use every means to escape. The government that stands aloof leaves power with the people. The government that steps in takes their power away. As one gains, the other loses. As one meets with happiness, the other encounters misery."

WANG P'ANG says, "All creatures share the same breath. But the movement of this breath comes and goes. It ends only to begin again. Hence, happiness and misery alternate like the seasons. But only sages realize this. Hence, in everything they do, they aim for the middle and avoid the extremes, unlike the government that insists on directness and goodness and forbids deception and evil, unlike the government that wants the world to be happy and yet remains unaware that happiness alternates with misery."

LU NUNG-SHIH says, "Only those who are free of directness can transcend the appearance of good and evil and eliminate happiness and misery. For they alone know where they end. Meanwhile, those who cannot reach the state where they aren't direct, who remain in the realm of good and evil, suffer happiness and misery as if they were on a wheel that carries them farther astray."

TE-CH'ING says, "The world withers, and the Tao fades. People are not the way they once were. They don't know directness from deception or good from evil. Even sages cannot instruct them. Hence, to transform them, sages enter their world of confusion. They join the dust of others and soften their own light. And they leave no trace."

WU CH'ENG says, "A sage's nonaction is nonaction that is not nonaction. Edges always cut. But the edge that is not an edge does not cut. Points always pierce. But the point that is not a point does not pierce. Lines always extend. But the line that is not a line does not extend. Lights always blind. But the light that is not a light does not blind. All of these are examples of nonaction."

In line thirteen, Mawangtui B omits *sheng-jen* (sage). Line fourteen also appears in the *Lichi*: "The gentleman compares his virtue to that of jade: pointed but not piercing." Line fifteen recalls verse 45: "perfectly straight it seems crooked." Wu Ch'eng combines this verse with the previous verse.

59

長生久視之道。
有國之母可以長久。是謂深根固柢。
無不剋則莫知其極。莫知其極可以有國。
早備是謂重積德。重積德則無不剋。
治人事天。莫若嗇。夫唯嗇是以早備。

In governing people and caring for Heaven
nothing surpasses economy
economy means planning ahead
planning ahead means accumulating virtue
accumulating virtue means overcoming all
overcoming all means knowing no limit
knowing no limit means guarding the realm
and guarding the realm's mother means living long
which means deep roots and a solid trunk
the Way of a long and lasting life

LI HSI-CHAI says, "Outside, we govern others. Inside, we care for Heaven. In both, nothing surpasses economy. Those who are economical are economical in everything. They are watchful within and on guard without. Only if we are still, does virtue have a place to collect."

MENCIUS says, "The way we care for Heaven is by guarding our mind and nourishing our nature" (*Mencius*: 7A.1).

WANG TAO says, "'Caring for Heaven' means preserving what one receives from Heaven. It means cultivating oneself."

Linking this with the previous verse, SU CH'E says, "Economy is the reason the edges of sages don't cut, their points don't pierce, their lines don't extend, and their lights don't blind. Economy means possessing without using."

WANG PI says, "Economy means farming. Farmers cultivate their fields by weeding out different species and concentrating on one. They don't worry about pulling out the withered and diseased. They pull out the causes of withering and disease. Above, they accept the will of Heaven. Below, they nourish others."

HAN FEI says, "Most people use their mind recklessly. Recklessness means waste, and waste means exhaustion. Sages use their mind calmly. Calmness means carefulness, and carefulness means economy. Economy is an art born of an understanding of the Tao. Those who know how to govern others calm their thoughts. Those who know how to care for Heaven clear their openings. When their thoughts are calm, old virtue remains within. When their openings are clear, new breath enters from without."

HO-SHANG KUNG says, "Someone whose virtue knows no limits can guard the gods of the realm and bring happiness to the people."

THE *LICHI* says, "Those who guard the realm are ever careful" (27).

LI JUNG says, "When rulers maintain the Tao, their countries are at peace. When they fail to maintain the Tao, their countries are in chaos. Their countries are the offspring. The Tao is their mother."

WU CH'ENG says, "The realm here is a metaphor for the body. Breath is the body's mother. Breath that has no limit can preserve the body. Those who fill themselves with breath can conquer the world and remain unharmed. Breath rises from below as if from the roots of a tree. By nourishing the roots, the roots grow deep. Breath flourishes above just as the trunk of a tree does. By nourishing the trunk, the trunk becomes firm. Thus, the tree doesn't wither."

LU NUNG-SHIH says, "The roots are in the dark, and the trunk is in the light. The roots refer to life, and the trunk refers to nature. What nothing can fathom is deep. Only life can match this. What nothing can topple is firm. Only nature can match this."

In line two, *shih* (pattern) appears in some editions instead of *se* (economy). I have followed the Fuyi and Suotan editions as well as the Kuotien texts and Mawangtui B in choosing the latter. Also, I have followed the Kuotien texts in preferring *pei* (prepare) in lines three and four over *fu* (subdue). The last line appears as a saying in other ancient texts, including *Hsuntzu: 4* and *Lushih Chunchiu: 1.3.* Where it does, commentators interpret *shih* (vision) as a cliché for "life," and I have followed suit here. Although the transition from matriarchal to patriarchal political forms took place in China sometime before the third millennium B.C., female deities have continued to dominate the pantheons of its folk and tribal regions.

60

夫　非　非　以　治
兩　其　其　道　大
不　神　鬼　蒞　國
相　不　不　天　。
傷　傷　神　下　若
。　人　。　。　烹
故　。　其　其　小
德　聖　神　鬼　鮮
交　人　不　不　。
歸　亦　傷　神
焉　不　人　。
。　傷　。
　　人
　　。

Ruling a great state
is like cooking a small fish
when you govern the world with the Tao
spirits display no powers
not that they have no powers
their powers don't harm the people
not that their powers can't harm
the sage keeps them from harming
and neither harms the other
for both rely on Virtue

In a poem bemoaning the absence of virtuous rulers, the SHIHCHING says, "Who can cook fish / I'll wash out the pot" (Kuei: 4).

LI HSI-CHAI says, "For the sage, ruling a state is a minor affair, like cooking a small fish."

HO-SHANG KUNG says, "If you cook a small fish, don't remove its entrails, don't scrape off its scales, and don't stir it. If you do, it will turn to mush. Likewise, too much government makes those below rebel. And too much cultivation makes one's vitality wither."

HAN FEI says, "In cooking a small fish, too much turning ruins it. In governing a great state, too much reform embitters the people. Thus, a ruler who possesses the Way values inaction over reform."

TE-CH'ING says, "A cruel government brings calamity down on the people. The people, however, think their suffering is the work of ghosts and spirits and turn to sacrifice and worship to improve their lot, when actually their misfortune is caused by their rulers."

THE TSOCHUAN says, "If the state is meant to flourish, listen to the people. If the state is meant to perish, listen to the spirits" (Chuang: 32).

WANG CHEN says, "The government that takes peace as its basis doesn't lose the Way. When the government doesn't lose the Way, *yin* and *yang* are in harmony. When *yin* and *yang* are in harmony, wind and rain arrive on time. When wind and rain arrive on time, the spirit world is at peace. When the spirit world is at peace, the legion of demons can't perform their sorcery."

WANG PI says, "Spirits don't injure what is natural. What is natural gives spirits no opening. When spirits have no opening, spirits cannot act like spirits."

CH'ENG HSUAN-YING says, "Spirits dwell in the *yin,* and people dwell in the *yang.* When both accept their lot, neither injures the other."

SU CH'E says, "The inaction of the sage makes people content with the way they are. Outside, nothing troubles them. Inside, nothing frightens them. Even spirits have no means of using their powers. It isn't that spirits have no powers. They have powers, but they don't use them to harm people. The reason people and spirits don't harm each other is because they look up to the sage. And the sage never harms anyone."

WU CH'ENG says, "The reason spirits don't harm the people is not because they can't but because the sage is able to harmonize the energy of the people so that they don't injure the energy of the spirit world. The reason neither injures the other is due to the sage's virtue. Hence, both worlds rely on the virtue of the sage."

HSUAN-TSUNG says, "'Neither' here refers to spirits and the sage."

LI JUNG says, "Spirits and sages help people without harming each other. One is hidden, the other manifest. But both rely on virtue."

SUNG CH'ANG-HSING says, "Spirits are spirits because they respond but can't be seen. Sages are sages because they govern but don't act. The virtue of sages and the virtue of spirits is the same."

Commenting on the *Taoteching* is also like cooking a small fish. Better to have left it in the sea. Commentators are divided as to whether the subjects of lines nine and ten are spirits and the people or spirits and the sage. Given the usual ambiguous syntax of the Chinese language, both are possible, but my reading gives the nod to spirits and sages.

61

大邦者下流。天下之交。天下之牝。牝恆以靜勝牡。

為其靜。故宜為下。大邦以下小邦。則取小邦。

小邦以下大邦。則取於大邦。故或下以取。或下而取。

故大邦者不過欲。兼畜人。小邦者不過欲。入事人。

夫皆得其欲。則大者宜為下。

A great state is a watershed
the confluence of the world
the female of the world
the female uses stillness to overcome the male
in order to be still
she needs to be lower
the great state that lowers itself before the small state
governs the small state
the small state that lowers itself before the great state
is governed by the great state
some lower themselves to govern
some lower themselves to be governed
the great state's one desire
is to unite and lead others
the small state's one desire
is to join and serve others
for both to fulfill their desires
whichever is greater needs to be lower

LAO-TZU says, "The reason the sea can govern a hundred rivers / is because it has mastered being lower" (*Taoteching*: 66).

HO-SHANG KUNG says, "To lead a great state, we should be like the sea. We should be at the bottom of a watershed and not fight even the smallest current. A great state is the meeting place of the high and the low. The female refers to everything *yin*, everything that is weak, humble, yielding—what doesn't lead."

TS'AO TAO-CH'UNG says, "The female is the mother. All creatures revere their mother. The sage recognizes the male but upholds the female. Hence, all creatures turn to the sage."

SU CH'E says, "The world turns to a great state just as rivers flow downstream. If a great state can lower itself, small states will attach themselves to it. If a small state can lower itself, a great state will take it under its care. A great state lowers itself to govern others. A small state lowers itself to be governed by others."

WU CH'ENG says, "The female doesn't make the first move. It is always the male who makes the first move. But to act means to lose the advantage. To wait means to gain the advantage. To act means to be higher. To wait means to be lower. The great state that doesn't presume on its superiority gains the voluntary support of the small state. The small state that is content with its inferiority enjoys the generosity of the great state. The small state doesn't have to worry about being lower, but the great state does. Hence, the great state needs to be lower."

WANG AN-SHIH says, "To serve someone greater is easy. To serve someone smaller is hard. Because it is hard, Lao-tzu says, 'whichever is greater needs to be lower.'"

MENCIUS says, "Only a virtuous ruler is able to serve a smaller state. Only a wise ruler is able to serve a greater state" (*Mencius*: 1B.3).

WANG PI says, "By cultivating humility, each gets what it wants. When the small state cultivates humility, it preserves itself, but that is all. It can't make the world turn to it. The world turns to the great state that cultivates humility. Thus, each gets what it wants. But it is the great state that needs to be more humble."

The Fuyi edition adds *t'ien-hsia-chih* (of the world) to line one, and the Mawang-tui texts invert lines two and three. I have decided against both variants. However, I have followed the Mawangtui texts in their wording of lines five and six and have followed them again, along with the Fuyi text, in their addition of the particle *yu* (by) to line ten. This variant clarifies a relationship between great and small that was previously ambiguous and easily misinterpreted.

62

道者萬物之奧。善人之寶。不善人之所保。美言可以市。尊行可以賀人之不善。何棄之有。故立天子。置三卿。雖有拱之璧。以先駟馬。不如坐而進此道。古之所以貴此道者。何不謂。求以得。有罪以勉與。故為天下貴。

The Tao is creation's sanctuary
treasured by the good
it keeps the bad alive
beautiful words might be the price
noble deeds might be the gift
how can we abandon
people who are bad
thus when emperors are enthroned
or ministers installed
though there be great disks of jade
followed by teams of horses
they don't rival one who sits
and offers up this Way
the ancients thus esteemed it
for did they not proclaim
who seeks thereby obtains
who errs thereby escapes
thus the world esteems it

THE *HSISHENGCHING* says, "The Tao is the sanctuary of the deepest depth and the source of empty nothingness."

WU CH'ENG says, "'Sanctuary' means the most honored place. The layout of ancestral shrines includes an outer hall and an inner chamber. The southwest corner of the inner chamber is called 'the sanctuary,' and the sanctuary is where the gods dwell."

SU CH'E says, "All we see of things is their exterior, their entrance hall. The Tao is their sanctuary. We all have one, but we don't see it. The wise alone are able to find it. Hence, Lao-tzu says the good treasure it, but the foolish don't find it. Then again, who doesn't the Tao protect? Hence, he says it protects the bad. The Tao doesn't abandon people. People abandon the Tao."

WANG PI says, "Beautiful words can excel the products of the marketplace. Noble deeds can elicit a response a thousand miles away."

TE-CH'ING says, "The Tao is in us all. Though good and bad might differ, our nature is the same. How, then, can we abandon anyone?"

LAO-TZU says, "Sages are good at saving others / therefore they abandon no one / nor anything of use / this is called cloaking the light / thus the good instruct the bad / the bad learn from the good" (*Taoteching*: 27).

WANG P'ANG says, "Jade disks and fine horses are used to attract talented people to the government. But a government that finds talented people yet does not implement the Tao is not followed by its subjects."

CHIANG HSI-CH'ANG says, "In ancient times, the less valuable presents came first. Hence, jade disks preceded horses."

LI HSI-CHAI says, "Better than disks of jade followed by teams of horses would be one good word or one good deed to keep the people from losing sight of the good."

LU NUNG-SHIH says, "If words and deeds can be offered to others, how much more the Tao."

WANG AN-SHIH says, "There is nothing that is not the Tao. When good people seek it, they are able to find it. When bad people seek it, they are able to avoid punishment."

In line one, both Mawangtui texts have *chu* (flow/chief) instead of *ao* (sanctuary). However, this is not supported by any other edition. In lines four and five, commentators have long suspected an error, and Mawangtui A has given us a partial solution. In line five, I have used its *ho-jen* (give to people) in place of the usual *chia-jen* (surpass people). However, I have deleted *jen* (people) as a copyist error for the word that begins line six. Note, though, that in my translation, I have inverted the order of lines six and seven.

63

為無為。事無事。味無味。大小多少。報怨以德。
圖難於其易。為大於其細。天下之難作於易。
天下之大作於細。是以聖人終不為大。
故能成其大。夫輕諾必寡信。多易必多難。
是以聖人猶難之。故終於無難。

Act without acting
work without working
understand without understanding
great or small many or few
repay each wrong with virtue
plan for the hard while it's easy
deal with the great while it's small
the world's hardest task begins easy
the world's greatest goal begins small
sages therefore never act great
they thus achieve great goals
who quickly agrees is seldom trusted
who thinks things easy finds them hard
sages therefore think everything hard
and thus find nothing hard

HO-SHANG KUNG says, "To act without acting means to do only what is natural. To work without working means to avoid trouble by preparing in advance. To understand without understanding means to understand the meaning of the Tao through meditation."

LI HSI-CHAI says, "When we act without acting, we don't exhaust ourselves. When we work without working, we don't trouble others. When we understand without understanding, we don't waste anything."

WANG TAO says, "What people do involves action. What sages do accords with the Tao of nonaction. 'Work' refers to the conditions of action. 'Understanding' refers to the meaning of action."

SUNG CH'ANG-HSING says, "To act without acting, to work without working, to understand without understanding is to conform with what is natural and not to impose oneself on others. Though others treat sages wrongly, the wrong is theirs and not the sages'. Sages respond with the virtue within their hearts. Utterly empty and detached, they thus influence others to trust in doing nothing."

CHIAO HUNG says, "Action involves form and thus includes great and small. It is also tied to number and thus includes many and few. This is where wrongs come from. Only the Tao is beyond form and beyond number. Thus, sages treat everything the same: great and small, many and few. Why should they respond to them with anger?"

TS'AO TAO-CH'UNG says, "If we repay wrongs with kindness, we put an end to revenge. If we repay wrongs with wrongs, revenge never ends."

HAN FEI says, "In terms of form, the great necessarily starts from the small. In terms of duration, the many necessarily starts from the few. Wise rulers detect small schemes and thus avoid great plots. They enact minor punishments and thus avoid major rebellions."

DUKE WEN OF CHIN told Kuo Yen, "In the beginning, I found it easy to rule the kingdom. Now I find it hard." Kuo Yen replied, "If you consider something easy, it is bound to become hard. If you consider something hard, it is bound to become easy" (*Kuoyu*: Chin.4).

WANG CHEN says, "If rulers disdain something as easy, misfortune and trouble are sure to arise from it. If they do not pay attention to small matters, eventually they will overwhelm even the greatest virtue. Thus, sages guard against the insignificant lest it amount to something great. If they wait until something is great before they act, their action will come too late."

TE-CH'ING says, "When I entered the mountains to cultivate the Way, at first it was very hard. But once I learned how to use my mind, it became very easy. What the world considers hard, the sage considers easy. What the world considers easy, the sage considers hard."

The Kuotien texts have only the first three lines and the last three lines of this verse. For my interpretation of *wei* in line three, I have followed that of *Wentzu*: 1, where line three appears as *chih-pu-chih*, "know without knowing." Normally, *wei* is taken to mean "taste." Lines ten and eleven also appear in verse 34, although my translation of them there is different.

64

其安易持。其未兆易謀。其脆易破。其微易散。為之於未有。治之於未亂。
合抱之木生於毫末。九成之臺起於累土。千里之行始於足下。為之者敗之。
執之者失之。是以聖人無為。故無敗。無執。故無失。民之從事。
恆於幾成而敗之。慎終如始。則無敗事矣。是以聖人欲不欲。
而不貴難得之貨。學不學。而復眾人之所過。以輔萬物之自然。而不敢為。

It's easy to rule while it's peaceful
it's easy to plan for before it appears
it's easy to break while it's fragile
it's easy to disperse while it's small
act before anything exists
govern before anyone rebels
a giant tree grows from the tiniest shoot
a great tower rises from a basket of dirt
a thousand-mile journey begins at your feet
but to act is to fail
to control is to lose
sages therefore don't act
thus they don't fail
they don't control
thus they don't lose
when people pursue a task
failure occurs near the end
care at the end as well as the start
means an end to failure
sages thus seek what no one else seeks
they don't prize hard-to-get goods
they study what no one else studies
they turn to what others pass by
to help all things remain natural
they dare not act

LU HUI-CH'ING says, "We should act before anything exists, while things are peaceful and latent. We should govern before anyone rebels, while they are weak and few. But to act before anything exists means to act without acting. To govern before anyone rebels means to govern without governing."

SU CH'E says, "To act before anything exists comes first. To govern before anyone rebels comes next."

KUAN-TZU says, "Know where success and failure lie, then act" (*Kuantzu*: 47).

HUAI-NAN-TZU says, "A needle creates a tapestry. A basket of earth makes a wall. Success and failure begin from something small" (*Huainantzu*: 16).

SUNG CH'ANG-HSING says, "From a sprout, the small becomes great. From a basket of earth, the low becomes high. From here, the near becomes far. But trees are cut down, towers are toppled, and journeys end. Everything we do eventually results in failure. Everything we control is eventually lost. But if we act before anything exists, how can we fail? If we govern before anyone rebels, how can we lose?"

WANG P'ANG says, "Everything has its course. When the time is right, it arrives. But people are blind to this truth and work to speed things up. They try to help Heaven and end up ruining things just as they near completion."

HO-SHANG KUNG says, "Others seek the ornamental. Sages seek the simple. Others seek form. Sages seek Virtue. Others study facts and skills. Sages study what is natural. Others learn how to govern the world. Sages learn how to govern themselves and how to uphold the truth of the Way."

HAN FEI says, "The wise don't fill their lessons with words or their shelves with books. The world may pass them by, but rulers turn to them when they want to learn what no one else learns."

WU CH'ENG says, "The sage seeks without seeking and studies without studying. For the truth of all things lies not in acting but in doing what is natural. By not acting, the sage shares in the naturalness of all things."

For line nine, the Mawangtui texts have: "a height of a hundred fathoms." There are two copies of the latter half of this verse among the Kuotien texts. In the first copy, line seventeen is omitted and line sixteen is *lin-shih-chih-chi*, "the rule for dealing with things." In the second copy, line sixteen is omitted but line seventeen is present, although after line eighteen and in variant form. In line twenty-two, the first Kuotien copy has *chiao* (teach), while the second has *hsueh* (study).

65

玄德深矣。遠矣。與物反矣。乃至大順。
恆知此兩者。亦稽式。恆知稽式。是謂玄德。
以其智。故以智治邦。邦之賊。不以智治邦。邦之德。
古之善為道者。非以明民。將以愚之。民之難治。

The ancient masters of the Way
tried not to enlighten
but to keep people in the dark
what makes people hard to rule
is their knowledge
who rules the realm with knowledge
is the terror of the realm
who rules without knowledge
is the paragon of the realm
who understands the difference
is one who finds the key
knowing how to find the key
is what we call Dark Virtue
Dark Virtue goes deep
goes far
goes the other way
until it reaches perfect harmony

WU CH'ENG says, "To make the people more natural, the ancient sages did not try to make the people more knowledgeable but to make them less knowledgeable. This radical doctrine was later misused by the First Emperor of the Ch'in dynasty, who burned all the books [in 213 B.C.] to make the people ignorant."

CHUANG-TZU says, "When the knowledge of bows and arrows arose, the birds above were troubled. When the knowledge of hooks and nets proliferated, the fish below were disturbed. When the knowledge of snares and traps spread, the creatures of the wild were bewildered. When the knowledge of argument and disputation multiplied, the people were confused. Thus are the world's troubles due to the love of knowledge" (*Chuangtzu*: 10.4).

WANG PI says, "When you rouse the people with sophistry, treacherous thoughts arise. When you counter their deceptions with more sophistry, the people see through your tricks and avoid them. Thus, they become secretive and devious."

LIU CHUNG-P'ING says, "Those who rule without knowledge turn to Heaven. Those who rule with knowledge turn to Humankind. Those who turn to Heaven are in harmony. Those who are in harmony do only what requires no effort. Their government is lenient. Those who turn to Humankind force things. Those who force things become lost in the Great Inquisition. Hence, their people are dishonest." Liu's terminology here is indebted to *Chuangtzu:* 19.2 and *Mencius:* 4B.26.

HO-SHANG KUNG says, "'Difference' refers to 'with knowledge' and 'without knowledge.' Once you know that knowledge spreads evil and lack of knowledge spreads virtue, you understand the key to cultivating the self and governing the realm. Once you understand the key, you share the same virtue as Heaven. And Heaven is dark. Those who possess Dark Virtue are so deep they can't be fathomed, so distant they can't be reached, and always do the opposite of others. They give to others, while others think only of themselves."

SUNG CH'ANG-HSING says, "Because it is so deep, you can't hear it or see it. Because it is so distant, you can't talk about it or reach it. Dark Virtue differs from everything else. But it agrees with the Tao."

SU CH'E says, "What the sage values is virtue. What others value is knowledge. Virtue and knowledge are opposites. Knowledge is seldom harmonious, while virtue is always harmonious."

LIN HSI-YI says, "'Perfect harmony' means whatever is natural."

Line one also begins verse 15. I have followed the Mawangtui texts in line six, where they omit *to* (too much), and also in line nine, where they replace *fu* (blessing) with *te* (virtue/paragon). This last variant also appears in *Wentzu:* 1. This verse is not present in the Kuotien texts.

66

The reason the sea can govern a hundred rivers
is because it has mastered being lower
thus it can govern a hundred rivers
hence if sages would be above the people
they should speak as if they were below them
if they would be in front
they should act as if they were behind them
thus when sages are above
the people aren't burdened
when they are in front
the people aren't obstructed
the world never wearies
of pushing sages forward
and because they don't struggle
no one can struggle against them

YEN TSUN says, "Rivers don't flow toward the sea because of its reputation or its power but because it does nothing and seeks nothing."

TE-CH'ING says, "All rivers flow toward the sea, regardless of whether they are muddy or clear. And the sea is able to contain them all because it is adept at staying below them. This is a metaphor for sages, to which the world turns because they are selfless."

LU HUI-CH'ING says, "When sages possess the kingdom, they speak of themselves as 'orphaned, widowed, and impoverished' or 'inheritor of the country's shame and misfortune.' Thus, in their speech, they place themselves below others. They do not act unless they are forced. They do not respond unless they are pushed. They do not rise unless they have no choice. Thus, in their actions, they place themselves behind others."

HO-SHANG KUNG says, "When sages rule over the people, they don't oppress those below with their position. Thus, the people uphold them and don't think of them as a burden. When sages stand before them, they don't blind them with their glory. Thus, the people love them as parents and harbor no resentment. Sages are kind and loving and treat the people as if they were their children. Thus, the whole world wants them for their leaders. The people never grow tired of them because sages don't struggle against them. Everyone struggles against something. But no one struggles against those who don't struggle against anything."

SU CH'E says, "Sages don't try to be above or in front of others. But when they find themselves below or behind others, the Tao can't help but lift them up and push them forward."

YANG HSIUNG says, "Those who hold themselves back are advanced by others. Those who lower themselves are lifted up by others" (*Fayen*: 7).

LI HSI-CHAI says, "The people aren't burdened when sages are above them, because the people aren't aware they have a ruler. And the people aren't obstructed when sages are before them, because sages aren't aware the people are their charges."

WANG CHEN says, "Through humility sages gain the approval of the people. Once they gain their approval, they gain their tireless support. And once they gain their tireless support, struggling over rank naturally comes to an end."

There is a relative lack of commentary for this verse. Wang Pi, for example, says nothing at all. The only textual issue is whether to read the last two lines as a statement or as a rhetorical question: "Is it not because they don't struggle / that no one can struggle against them?" The Mawangtui and Fuyi texts word them as a question, while the Suotan and Wangpi versions, which I have followed, word them as a statement. Both lines also appear as a statement in verse 22. This verse is not present in the Kuotien texts.

67

天下皆謂我大。大而似不肖。夫唯大故不肖。若肖。久矣其細。

夫我恆有三寶。持而寶之。一曰慈。二曰儉。三曰不敢為天下先。

夫慈。故能勇。儉。故能廣。不敢為天下先。故能成器長。

今捨其慈且勇。舍其儉且廣。舍其後且先。則死矣。

夫慈以戰則勝。以守則固。天將建之。以慈垣之。

The world calls me great
great but useless
it's because I am great I am useless
if I were of use
I would have remained small
but I possess three treasures
I treasure and uphold
first is compassion
second is austerity
third is reluctance to excel
because I'm compassionate
I can be valiant
because I'm austere
I can be extravagant
because I'm reluctant to excel
I can be chief of all tools
if I renounced compassion for valor
austerity for extravagance
humility for superiority
I would die
but compassion wins every battle
and outlasts every attack
what Heaven creates
let compassion protect

HO-SHANG KUNG says, "Lao-tzu says the world calls his virtue 'great.' But if his virtue were great in name alone, it would bring him harm. Hence, he acts foolish and useless. He doesn't distinguish or differentiate. Nor does he demean others or glorify himself."

WANG PI says, "To be useful is to lose the means to be great."

SU CH'E says, "The world honors daring, exalts ostentation, and emphasizes progress. What the sage treasures is patience, frugality, and humility, all of which the world considers useless."

TE-CH'ING says, "'Compassion' means to embrace all creatures without reservation. 'Austerity' means not to exhaust what one already has. 'Reluctance to excel' means to drift through the world without opposing others."

WANG AN-SHIH says, "Through compassion, we learn to be soft. When we are soft, we can overcome the hardest thing in the world. Thus, we can be valiant. Through austerity, we learn when to stop. When we know when to stop, we are always content. Thus, we can be extravagant. Through reluctance to excel, we are surpassed by no one. Thus, we can be chief of all tools. Valor, extravagance, and excellence are what everyone worries about. And because they worry, they are always on the verge of death."

LIU SHIH-P'EI says, "To be chief of all tools means to be the chief official." (For "chief of all tools," see verse 28.)

CONFUCIUS says, "The gentleman is not a tool" (*Lunyu*: 2.12).

WU CH'ENG says, "Compassion is the chief of the three treasures. The last section only mentions compassion because it includes the other two. All people love a compassionate person as they do their own parents. How could anyone oppose their parents? Hence, those who attack or defend with compassion meet no opposition."

MENCIUS says, "Those who are kind have no enemy under Heaven" (*Mencius:* 7B.3).

To be a tool means to be limited. To have no limits means to be chief of all tools. Among compassion, austerity, and reluctance to excel, only compassion has no limits. Hence, Lao-tzu ranks it first. Line one of the Wangpi edition reads: "The world calls my Tao great." But the word *tao* does not appear in the Fuyi or Suotan editions or in the Mawangtui texts. Thus, I have omitted it. In line sixteen, Han Fei and Mawangtui A have *ch'eng-shih,* "chief of those who succeed." But there is no other support for this variant. Finally, for the penultimate line, I have followed the Mawangtui version, which has *chien* (create) instead of the usual *chiu* (save). This verse is not present in the Kuotien texts.

68

古之。善為士者不武。
善戰者不怒。善勝敵者不與。
善用人者為之下。
是謂不爭之德。是謂用人之力。
是謂配天。古之極。

In ancient times
the perfect officer wasn't armed
the perfect warrior wasn't angry
the perfect victor wasn't hostile
the perfect commander acted humble
this is the virtue of nonaggression
this is using the strength of others
this is uniting with Heaven
which was the ancient end

CHIAO HUNG says, "In ancient times, officers went into battle in chariots. They were dressed in mail, and there were three to a vehicle: one on the left armed with a bow, one on the right armed with a spear, and one in the middle in charge of the reins, the flag, and the drum. Below and arrayed around every chariot were seventy-two foot soldiers."

SUN-TZU says, "A ruler must not mobilize his armies in anger. A general must not engage the enemy in wrath. Anger can turn to joy, and wrath can turn to gladness. But once a state is destroyed, it cannot be restored. And once a person is dead, he cannot be reborn" (*Suntzu Pingfa*: 12.18–21). Sun-tzu also says, "To win every battle is not supreme excellence. Supreme excellence is to conquer without fighting" (3.2).

HO-SHANG KUNG says, "Those who honor the Way and Virtue are not fond of weapons. They keep hatred from their hearts. They eliminate disaster before it arises. They are angered by nothing. They use kindness among neighbors and virtue among strangers. They conquer their enemies without fighting and command through humility."

LIEH-TZU says, "Those who govern others with worthiness never win them over. Those who serve others with worthiness never fail to gain their support" (*Liehtzu*: 6.3).

WANG CHEN says, "You must first win others' hearts before you can command them."

KUMARAJIVA says, "Empty your body and mind. No one can fight against nothing."

WU CH'ENG says, "Even though our wisdom and power might surpass that of others, we should act as if we possessed neither. By making ourselves lower than others, we can use their wisdom and power as our own. Thus, we can win without taking up arms, without getting angry, and without making enemies. By using the virtue of nonaggression and the power of others, we are like Heaven, which overcomes without fighting and which reaches its goal without moving."

TZU-SSU says, "Wide and deep, they are able to support others. High and bright, they are able to protect others. Those who are wide and deep unite with Earth. Those who are high and bright unite with Heaven" (*Chungyung:* 26.4–5).

TE-CH'ING says, "Heaven is *yang* and Earth is *yin*. But if Heaven and Earth remain stationary, everything stops, and nothing comes into existence. Only when *yang* descends and *yin* rises does everything flourish. Thus, Heaven's position is to be above, but its function is to descend. When sages are above the people, and their hearts are below, we call this uniting with Heaven. This was the polestar of ancient rulers."

Some editions drop the opening phrase, *ku-chih* (ancient times), and combine this with the previous verse. I have followed the Fuyi edition in retaining it. Mawangtui B has *ku* (thus). In line seven, both Mawangtui texts omit the phrase *chih-li,* "the strength of," but no other edition follows suit. Finally, some later commentators read the last two lines as one line, eliminating *ku* (ancient) as a copyist error: "We call this the end of uniting with Heaven." But this is not supported by any early text or commentary. This verse is not present in the Kuotien texts.

69

故抗兵相若。則哀者勝矣。
禍莫大於無敵。無敵近亡吾寶。
攘無臂。執無兵。扔無敵。
不敢進寸。而退尺。是謂行無行。
用兵有言曰。吾不敢為主。而為客。

In warfare there is a saying
rather than a host
better to be a guest
rather than advance an inch
better to retreat a foot
this means to form no ranks
to put on no armor
to brandish no weapons
to repulse no enemy
no fate is worse than to have no enemy
to have no enemy is to lose one's treasure
thus when opponents are evenly matched
the remorseful one prevails

WANG CHEN says, "In warfare, we say the one who mobilizes first is the host and the one who responds is the guest. Sages only go to war when they have no choice. Hence, they are the guest."

CHIAO HUNG says, "This was a saying of ancient military strategists." If so, they remain unnamed. Sun-tzu, meanwhile, calls the invading force the k'o (guest) (*Suntzu Pingfa*: 2.20).

HO-SHANG KUNG says, "According to the Tao of warfare, we should avoid being the first to mobilize troops, and we should go to war only after receiving Heaven's blessing."

LU HUI-CH'ING says, "The host resists, and the guest agrees. The host toils, and the guest relaxes. One advances with pride, while the other retreats in humility. One advances with action, while the other retreats in quiet. Those who meet resistance with agreement, toil with relaxation, pride with humility, and action with stillness have no enemy. Wherever they go, they conquer."

SUNG CH'ANG-HSING says, "In warfare, sages leave no tracks. They advance by retreating."

WU CH'ENG says, "Those who go to war form themselves into ranks, equip themselves with weapons, and advance against the enemy. But when sages go to war, they act as if there were no ranks, there were no armor, there were no weapons, and as if there were no enemies."

SUN-TZU says, "Generals who advance with no thought of fame, who retreat with no fear of punishment, who think only of protecting their country and helping their king are the treasures of the realm" (*Suntzu Pingfa:* 10.24).

SU CH'E says, "Sages regard compassion as their treasure. To treat killing lightly would be to lose the reason for compassion."

TE-CH'ING says, "When opponents are evenly matched and neither is superior, the winner is hard to determine. But whichever one is remorseful and compassionate will win. For the Way of Heaven is to love life and to help those who are compassionate to overcome their enemies."

WANG PI says, "Those who are remorseful sympathize with their opponents. They try not to gain an advantage but to avoid injury. Hence, they always win."

WANG P'ANG says, "To be remorseful is to be compassionate. Those who are compassionate are able to be courageous. Thus, they triumph."

LIN HSI-YI says, "Those who attack with drums and cheer the advent of war are not remorseful. They are remorseful who do not consider warfare a pleasure but an occasion for mourning. In this verse, warfare is only a metaphor for the Tao."

LAO-TZU says, "When you kill another / honor him with your tears / when the battle is won / treat it as a wake" (*Taoteching:* 31).

The import of lines ten and eleven would seem to be that without an enemy, we would have no recipient of our compassion and thus no reason to practice it. The standard editions reverse the order of lines eight and nine. In lines ten and eleven, they also have *ch'ing-ti* (treat enemies lightly) in place of *wu-ti* (have no enemies). And in line twelve, they have *hsiang-chia* (meet each other) in place of *hsiang-juo* (evenly matched). In all three cases, I have followed the Mawang-tui and Fuyi editions. The meaning of the last four lines becomes clearer if this verse is read as a continuation of the previous two verses. In verse 67, for example, Lao-tzu's "treasures" include compassion, austerity, and reluctance to excel. This verse is not present in the Kuotien texts.

70

吾言甚易知。甚易行。
而人莫之能知。莫之能行。
言有宗。事有君。夫唯無知。
是以不我知。知我者希。
則我貴矣。是以聖人被褐。而懷玉。

My words are easy to understand
and easy to practice
but no one understands them
or puts them into practice
words have an ancestor
deeds have a master
the reason I'm not understood
it's me who isn't understood
but because so few understand me
thus am I esteemed
sages therefore wear coarse cloth
and keep their jade concealed

TS'AO TAO-CH'UNG says, "Nothing is simpler or easier than the Tao. But because it's so simple, it can't be explained by reasoning. Hence, no one can understand it. And because it's so near, it can't be reached by stages. Hence, no one can put it into practice."

WANG P'ANG says, "Because sages teach us to be in harmony with the course of our lives, their words are simple, and their deeds are ordinary. Those who look within themselves understand. Those who follow their own nature do what is right. Difficulties arise when we turn away from the trunk and look among the branches."

LI HSI-CHAI says, "The Tao is easy to understand and easy to put into practice. It is also hard to understand and hard to put into practice. It is easy because there is no Tao to discuss, no knowledge to learn, no effort to make, no deeds to perform. And it is hard because the Tao cannot be discussed, because all words are wrong, because it cannot be learned, and because the mind only leads us astray. Effortless stillness is not necessarily right, and actionless activity is not necessarily wrong. This is why it is hard."

SU CH'E says, "Words can trap the Tao, and deeds can reveal its signs. But if the Tao could be found in words, we would have only to listen to words. And if it could be seen in deeds, we would only have to examine deeds. But it cannot be found in words or seen in deeds. Only if we put aside words and look for their ancestor and put aside deeds and look for their master, can we find it."

WU CH'ENG says, "The ancestor unites the clan. The master governs the state. Softness and humility are the ancestor of all words and the master of all deeds."

YEN TSUN says, "Wild geese fly for days but don't know what exists beyond the sky. Officials and scholars work for years, but none of them knows the extent of the Way. It's beyond the ken and beyond the reach of narrow-minded, one-sided people."

LU HUI-CH'ING says, "The reason the Tao is esteemed by the world is because it cannot be known or perceived. If it could be known or perceived, why should it be esteemed? Hence, Lao-tzu is esteemed because so few understand him. Thus, sages wear an embarrassed, foolish expression and seldom show anyone their great and noble virtue."

HO-SHANG KUNG says, "The reason people don't understand me is because my virtue is dark and not visible from the outside."

CONFUCIUS says, "I study what is below and understand what is above. Who knows me? Only Heaven" (*Lunyu*: 14.37).

WANG PI says, "To wear coarse cloth is to become one with what is ordinary. To keep one's jade concealed is to treasure the truth. Sages are difficult to know because they do not differ from ordinary people and because they do not reveal their treasure of jade."

Words and deeds can be falsified, but not understanding and practice. In my translation, I have inverted lines seven and eight. In line ten, the word *tse* (thus) can also mean "follow," and some commentators read the line: "Who follows me is esteemed." As with geodes, jade is found inside ordinary looking rocks. Officials once wore it on their hats as an emblem of their status, and alchemists often included it in their elixirs. This verse is not present in the Kuotien texts.

71

知不知尚矣。不知知病矣。是以聖人之不病。以其病病。是以不病。

To understand yet not understand
is transcendence
not to understand yet understand
is affliction
the reason sages aren't afflicted
is because they treat affliction as affliction
hence they aren't afflicted

CONFUCIUS says, "Shall I teach you about understanding? To treat understanding as understanding and to treat not-understanding as not-understanding, this is understanding" (*Lunyu*: 2.17).

TE-CH'ING says, "The ancients said that the word *understanding* was the door to all mysteries as well as the door to all misfortune. If you realize that you don't understand, you eliminate false understanding. This is the door to all mysteries. If you cling to understanding while trying to discover what you don't understand, you increase the obstacles to understanding. This is the door to all misfortune."

WU CH'ENG says, "Those who understand yet seem not to understand are the wisest of people. They protect their understanding with stupidity. Those who don't understand yet think they understand are, in fact, the stupidest of people. They think blind eyes see and deaf ears hear. This is what is meant by 'affliction.'"

TS'AO TAO-CH'UNG says, "If people understand, but out of humility they say they don't, then reality is superior to name. Hence, we call it transcendence. If people don't understand but say they do, then name surpasses reality. Hence, we call this affliction. Those who are able to understand that affliction is affliction are never afflicted."

SU CH'E says, "The Tao is not something that can be reached through reasoning. Hence, it cannot be understood. Those who do not yet understand do not understand that there is no entrance. And if they do understand, and then they think about their understanding, they become afflicted by understanding."

CHIAO HUNG says, "Anything that is understood is a delusion. Anything that is a delusion is an affliction. Understanding is not the affliction. It is the understanding of understanding that becomes the affliction. To understand what is the affliction is to cure the illness without medicine."

LI HSI-CHAI says, "Understanding depends on things. Hence, it involves fabrication. Not understanding returns to the origin. Hence, it approaches the truth. Those who can understand that not understanding approaches the truth and that understanding involves fabrication are transcendent. If they don't understand that understanding involves fabrication and vainly increase their understanding, they use the affliction as the medicine. Only by understanding that understanding is affliction can one be free of affliction. This is why sages are not afflicted."

HO-SHANG KUNG says, "To understand the Tao yet to say that we don't is the transcendence of virtue. Not to understand the Tao and to say that we do is the affliction of virtue. Lesser people don't understand the meaning of the Tao and vainly act according to their forced understanding and thereby harm their spirit and shorten their years. Sages don't suffer the affliction of forced understanding because they are pained by the affliction of others."

Thus do Zen masters ask their students to show them their original face, their face before they were born. The Fuyi and Wangpi editions include two additional lines between lines four and five: "To treat affliction as affliction / is to be unafflicted." But this would make the last lines more redundant than they already are. Neither line is included by Han Fei or found in the Mawangtui texts, the Chinglung edition, and at least two of our Tunhuang copies. Hence, I have not included them. This verse is not present in the Kuotien texts.

72

自愛。而不自貴。故去彼。而取此。
是以聖人自知。而不自見。
夫唯弗厭。是以不厭。
勿狹其所居。勿厭其所生。
民之不畏畏。則大畏將之矣。

When people no longer fear authority
a greater authority will appear
don't restrict where people dwell
don't repress how people live
if they aren't repressed
they won't protest
sages therefore know themselves
but don't reveal themselves
they love themselves
but don't exalt themselves
thus they pick this over that

WU CH'ENG says, "The authority we fear is what shortens years and takes lives. The 'greater authority' is our greater fear, namely death. When people no longer fear what they ought to fear, they advance their own death until the greater fear finally appears."

WANG P'ANG says, "When people are simple and their lives are good, they fear authority. But when those above lose the Way and enact all sorts of measures to restrict the livelihood of those below, people respond with deceit and are no longer subdued by authority. When this happens, natural calamities occur and misfortunes arise."

WANG CHEN says, "When ordinary officials and the common people have no fear, punishment occurs. When ministers and high officials have no fear, banishment occurs. When princes and kings have no fear, warfare occurs."

WEI YUAN says, "'Where people dwell' refers to conditions such as wealth and poverty. 'How people live' refers to physical activities, such as toil and rest. When people think that their dwellings or lives are not as good as others', they feel embarrassed and thus restricted, restricted and thus repressed. And when they feel repressed, they protest against 'this' and seek 'that,' not knowing that once their desire is fulfilled, what they fear comes close behind."

WANG PI says, "In tranquillity and peace is where we should dwell. Humble and empty is how we should live. But when we forsake tranquillity to pursue desires and abandon humility for authority, creatures are disturbed, and people are distressed. When authority cannot restore order, and people cannot endure authority, the link between those above and those below is severed, and natural calamities occur."

HO-SHANG KUNG says, "They know what they have and what they don't have. They don't display their virtue outside but keep it hidden inside. They love their body and protect their essence and breath. They don't exalt or glorify themselves before the world. 'That' refers to showing and glorifying themselves. 'This' refers to knowing and loving themselves."

TS'AO TAO-CH'UNG says, "'That' refers to external things. 'This' refers to one's inner reality."

Authority refers to a power outside us. Sages aren't concerned with acquiring or exercising such a power. The power of sages arises naturally from the cultivation of themselves. Lao tzu begins this verse with two puns. The force of the first pun in lines one and two is somewhat weakened in the Wangpi and other standard editions by the use of different homophones for "fear" and "authority." In his edition of 1587, Chiao Hung noted that in ancient times these characters were interchangeable, and he suggested using one for both words. This is, in fact, what occurs in the second pun in lines five and six, where the same character is used for "repress" and "protest." The Mawangtui texts, it turns out, agree with Chiao Hung, and I have amended lines one and two accordingly. In lines three and four, I have also turned to the Mawangtui texts for the negative injunction *wu* (don't). Other editions have *wu* (has not) or *pu* (does not), both of which result in problems regarding the referent and thus in different interpretations of the entire verse. The last line also occurs at the end of verses 12 and 38. This verse is not present in the Kuotien texts.

73

天網恢恢。疏而不失。
不言而善應。不召而自來。繟而善謀。
執知其故。天之道。
此兩者。或利。或害。天之所惡。
勇於敢則殺。勇於不敢則活。

Daring to act means death
daring not to act means life
of these two
one benefits
the other harms
what Heaven dislikes
who knows the reason
the Way of Heaven
is to win without a fight
to answer without a word
to come without a summons
and to plan without a thought
the Net of Heaven is all-embracing
its mesh is wide but nothing escapes

LI HSI-CHAI says, "Everyone knows about daring to act but not about daring not to act. Those who dare to act walk on the edge of a knife. Those who dare not to act walk down the middle of a path. Of these two, walking on a knife-edge is harmful, but people ignore the harm. Walking down the middle of a path is beneficial, but people are not aware of the benefit. Thus it is said, 'People can walk on the edge of a knife but not down the middle of a path'" (*Chungyung*: 9).

SU CH'E says, "Those who dare to act die. Those who dare not to act live. This is the normal pattern of things. But sometimes those who act live, and sometimes those who don't act die. What happens in the world depends on fortune. Sometimes what should happen doesn't. The Way of Heaven is far off. Who knows where its likes and dislikes come from?"

SUNG CH'ANG-HSING says, "The mechanism whereby some live and others die is obscure and hard to fathom. If sages find it difficult to know, what about ordinary people?"

YEN TSUN says, "Heaven does not consider life in its schemes or death in its work. It is impartial."

LU NUNG-SHIH says, "Loosely viewed, the hard and the strong conquer the soft and the weak. Correctly viewed, the soft and the weak conquer the hard and the strong. Hence, the hard and the strong are what Heaven dislikes."

WU CH'ENG says, "Because sages do not kill others lightly, evildoers slip through their nets, but not through the Net of Heaven. Heaven does not use its strength to fight against evildoers as Humanity does, and yet it always triumphs. It does not speak with a mouth as Humanity does, and yet it answers faster than an echo. It does not have to be summoned but arrives on its own. Evil has its evil reward. Even the clever cannot escape. Heaven is unconcerned and unmindful, but its retribution is ingenious and beyond the reach of human plans. It never lets evildoers slip through its net. Sages do not have to kill evildoers. Heaven will do it for them."

WANG AN-SHIH says, "*Yin* and *yang* take turns. The four seasons come and go. The moon waxes and wanes. All things have their time. They don't have to be summoned to come."

LI HUNG-FU says, "It wins because it doesn't fight. It answers because it doesn't speak. It comes because it isn't summoned. If it had to fight to win, something would escape, even if its mesh were fine."

After line seven, the Fuyi, Suotan, and Wangpi editions have: "Thus, even sages find it hard." However, this line does not appear in the Mawangtui, Chinglung, or Suichou editions, Tunhuang copies P.2347, P.2517, S.6543, or the Yentsun text. Ma Hsu-lun considers it an interpolation from verse 63, where it also appears, and I tend to agree. The last two lines have become a proverb in China. This verse is not present in the Kuotien texts.

74

夫代大匠斲。則希有不傷其手。　夫代司殺者殺。是代大匠斲。　夫執敢殺者。　若使民恆畏死。民恆必畏死。則恆有司殺者。　若民恆不畏死。奈何以殺懼之。若使民恆畏死。而為奇者。吾將得而殺之。

If people no longer fear death
what good is threatening to kill them
if people truly fear death
and some act perverse
and we catch and kill them
who else would dare
as long as people fear death
the executioner will exist
to kill in the executioner's place
is to cut in the carpenter's place
those who cut in the carpenter's place
seldom escape with hands intact

YIN WEN says, "Lao-tzu asks, if people are not afraid to die what good is threatening to kill them? If people are not afraid to die, it is because punishments are excessive. When punishments are excessive, people don't care about life. When they don't care about life, the ruler's might means nothing to them. When punishments are moderate, people are afraid to die. They are afraid to die because they enjoy life. When you know they enjoy life, then you can threaten them with death" (*Yinwen*: 2).

LI HSI-CHAI says, "This implies that punishments cannot be relied upon for governing. If people are not afraid of death, what use is threatening them with execution? And if they are afraid of death, and we catch someone who breaks the law, and we execute them, by killing one person we should be able to govern the rest. But the more people we kill, the more people break the law. Thus, punishment is not the answer."

MING T'AI-TSU says, "When I first ascended the throne, the people were unruly and officials corrupt. If ten people were executed in the morning, a hundred were breaking the same law by evening. Being ignorant of the Way of the ancient sage kings, I turned to the *Taoteching*. When I read, 'If people no longer fear death / what good is threatening to kill them,' I decided to do away with capital punishment and put criminals to work instead. In the year since then, the burdens of my heart have been lightened. Truly, this book is the greatest teacher of kings."

WU CH'ENG says, "'Perverse' means 'unlawful.' If those who act perverse and break the law do not meet with misfortune at the hands of Humankind, they will certainly be punished by Heaven."

HO-SHANG KUNG says, "If rulers teach according to the Tao and people respond with perversion instead, rulers are within their rights to arrest them and kill them. Lao-tzu, however, was concerned that rulers should use the Tao first before turning to punishment."

LU HUI-CH'ING says, "The meaning of 'the executioner will exist' is the same as 'the Net of Heaven is all-embracing / its mesh is wide but nothing escapes' [verse 73]. The executioner is Heaven."

SU CH'E says, "Heaven is the executioner. If the world is at peace and people engage in perversity and rebellion, then surely they have been abandoned by Heaven. If we kill them, it is Heaven who kills them and not us. But if we kill those whom Heaven has not abandoned, we take the executioner's place. And anyone who takes the executioner's place puts themselves within reach of his ax."

THE *LUSHIH CHUNCHIU* says, "A great carpenter does not cut" (1.4).

MENCIUS says, "The wise are not alone in desiring something greater than life and hating something greater than death. This is true of everyone. But the wise don't forget it" (*Mencius*: 6A.10).

Line seven appears only in the Mawangtui texts, but it seems needed to complete the meaning of line eight. At the end of line eight, the Fuyi and Wangpi editions add an extra *sha* (kill). I have followed the Suotan, Chingfu, and Mawangtui texts in omitting it. This verse is not present in the Kuotien texts.

75

民之飢。以其上食稅之多。是以飢。民之難治。以其上之有為。是以難治。民之輕死。以其上求生之厚。是以輕死。夫唯無以生為者。是賢於貴生。

The reason people are hungry
is that those above levy so many taxes
this is why they are hungry
the reason people are hard to rule
is that those above are so forceful
this is why they are hard to rule
the reason people think little of death
is that those above think so much of life
this is why they think little of death
meanwhile those who do nothing to live
are more esteemed than those who love life

DUKE AI approached YU JUO: "The year is one of famine, and my revenues are wanting. What am I to do?" Yu Juo replied, "Return to the 10 percent rate of taxation." Duke Ai said, "But I cannot get by on 20 percent. How will I survive on 10 percent?" Yu Juo replied, "When the people don't want, why should the ruler want. When the people want, why should the ruler not want?" (*Lunyu*: 12.9).

WANG PI says, "The people hide and disorder prevails because of those above, not because of those below. The people follow those above."

LI HSI-CHAI says, "If those above take too much, those below will be impoverished. If those above use too much force, those below will rebel. This is a matter of course. When people think their own life is more important, and they disregard the lives of others, why should others not treat death lightly? Sages don't think about life unless they are forced to."

TE-CH'ING says, "Robbers and thieves arise from hunger and cold. If people are hungry and have no means to live, they have no choice but to steal. When people steal, it's because those above force them. They force people to turn to stealing and then try to rule with cleverness and laws. But the more laws they make, the more thieves appear. Even the threat of the executioner's ax doesn't frighten them. And the reason people aren't frightened by death is that those above are so concerned with life."

SU CH'E says, "When those above use force to lead the people, the people respond with force. Thus do complications multiply and the people become hard to rule."

WANG CHEN says, "'Forceful' refers to the ruler's love of might and arms. But once arms prevail, disorder is certain."

HUAI-NAN-TZU says, "The reason people cannot live out their allotted years and are sentenced to death in midlife is that they think so much of life. Meanwhile, those who do nothing to stay alive are able to lengthen their lives" (*Huainantzu: 7*).

HO-SHANG KUNG says, "Only those who do nothing to stay alive, who aren't moved by titles or sinecures, who aren't affected by wealth or advantages, who refuse to serve the emperor or run errands for lesser lords—they alone are more esteemed than those who love life."

YEN TSUN says, "The Natural Way always turns things upside down. What has no body lives. What has a body dies. To be alive and to seek advantages is the beginning of death. Not to be alive and to get rid of advantages is the beginning of life. Those who don't work to live live long."

WANG TAO says, "The meaning of the last two lines is: If I didn't have this body of mine, what worries would I have?"

WANG P'ANG says, "If you understand only one of these three, you can understand the other two."

In line eight, I have followed the Fuyi edition in reading *ch'i-shang* (those above). Other editions have simply *ch'i* (those), leaving the referent in doubt. This verse is not present in the Kuotien texts.

76

兵強則滅。木強則折。堅強居下。柔弱居上。

故曰。堅強者死之徒也。柔弱者生之徒也。

草木之生也。柔脆。其死也。枯槁。

人之生也。柔弱。其死也。堅強。

When people are born
they are soft and weak
when they perish
they are hard and stiff
when plants shoot forth
they are supple and tender
when they die
they are withered and dry
thus is it said
the hard and stiff are followers of death
the soft and weak are followers of life
when an army becomes stiff it suffers defeat
when a plant becomes stiff it snaps
the hard and stiff dwell below
the soft and weak dwell above

HO-SHANG KUNG says, "When people are born, they contain breath and spirit. This is why they are soft. When they die, their breath ceases and their spirit disappears. This is why they are hard."

WU CH'ENG says, "Seeing that the living are soft and the dead are hard, we can infer that those whose virtue is hard and those whose actions are forceful die before their time, while those who are soft and weak are able to preserve their lives."

LI HSI-CHAI says, "Although the soft and weak aren't the same as the Tao, they approach its absence of effort. Hence, they aren't far from the Tao. Although the hard and stiff aren't outside the Tao, they involve effort. Hence, they lead people away from it."

LIEH-TZU says, "The world has a path of perennial victory and a path of perennial defeat. The path of perennial victory is weakness. The path of perennial defeat is strength. These two are easy to recognize, but people remain oblivious to them" (*Liehtzu*: 2.17).

LAO-TZU says, "The weak conquer the strong" (*Taoteching*: 36).

WANG CHEN says, "It isn't hard for an army to achieve victory. But it is hard to hold on to victory. There is no great army that has not brought on its own defeat through its victories."

HSI T'UNG says, "When a plant becomes stiff, it loses its flexibility and becomes easy to break."

WANG P'ANG says, "In terms of *yin* and *yang*, *yin* comes before and *yang* comes after. In terms of Heaven and Earth, Heaven is exalted and Earth is humble. In terms of Virtue, the soft and weak overcome the hard and stiff. But in terms of material things, the hard and stiff control the soft and weak. The people of this world only see things. They don't understand Virtue."

SU CH'E says, "As long as it contains empty breath, the body does not suffer from rigidity. As long as they reflect perfect reason, actions are not burdened by severity. According to the unchanging principle of things, the refined rises to the top, while the coarse sinks to the bottom. The refined is soft and weak, while the coarse is hard and stiff."

LI JUNG says, "The living belong above. The dead belong below."

How different this world would be if our leaders spent as much time in their gardens as they do in their war rooms. In line five, most editions include the phrase *wan-wu* (ten thousand creatures) before *ts'ao-wu* (plants). Chiang Hsi-ch'ang thinks, in light of the plant-specific adjectives of lines six and eight, this must be an interpolation, and I agree. It does not appear in the Yentsun or Fuyi editions. In line nine, I have relied on the Mawangtui texts for the addition of *yueh* (it is said). In line thirteen, I have turned to *Liehtzu*: 2.17, *Huainantzu*: 1, and *Wentzu*: 1 for *che* (snap). The Suotan and Fuyi editions have the puzzling *kung* (together), while the Wangpi edition has the equally strange *ping* (army), and the two Mawangtui texts offer no help with *keng* (end) and *ching* (compete), respectively. This verse is not present in the Kuotien texts.

77

天之道。其猶張弓乎。高者抑之。下者舉之。
有餘者損之。不足者補之。天之道。損有餘。
而補不足。人之道則不然。損不足。以奉有餘。
孰能有餘。以奉天下。其唯有道者乎。
是以聖人為而不恃。成功而不居。若此其不欲見賢耶。

The Way of Heaven
is like stringing a bow
pulling down the high
lifting up the low
shortening the long
lengthening the short
the Way of Heaven
takes from the long
and supplements the short
unlike the Way of Humankind
which takes from the short
and gives to the long
who can take the long
and give it to the world
only those who possess the Way
thus do sages not depend on what they develop
or claim what they achieve
thus they choose to hide their skill

KAO HENG says, "In stringing a bow, we pull the bow down to attach the string to the top. We lift the bow up to attach the string to the bottom. If the string is too long, we make it shorter. If the string is too short, we make it longer. This is exactly the Way of Heaven." My reading of line two, which agrees with Kao Heng's, is based on the *Shuowen*, which says, "*Chang* means to attach a string to a bow."

TU ER-WEI says, "Not only the Chinese, but the ancient Greeks and Hindus, the Finns, the Pawnee, and the Arapaho all likened the moon to a bow. Thus the Way of Heaven is like a bow" (*Lao-tzu-te-yueh-shen tsung-chiao*, pp. 97–98).

HO-SHANG KUNG says, "The Way of Heaven is so dark, we need metaphors to understand it. To prepare a bow for use, we string it by pulling down the top and lifting up the bottom. Likewise, the Way of Heaven is to take from the strong and give to the weak."

LU HUI-CH'ING says, "The Way of Heaven does not intentionally pull down the high and lift up the low. It does nothing and relies instead on the nature of things. Things that are high and long cannot avoid being pulled down and shortened. Things that are low and short cannot avoid being lifted up and lengthened. The full suffer loss. The humble experience gain."

TE-CH'ING says, "The Way of Heaven is to give but not to take. The Way of Humankind is to take but not to give."

WANG P'ANG says, "The Way of Heaven is based on the natural order. Hence, it is fair. The Way of Humankind is based on desire. Hence, it is not fair. Those who possess the Way follow the same Way as Heaven."

SU CH'E says, "Those who possess the Way supply the needs of the ten thousand creatures without saying a word. Only those who possess the Way are capable of this."

LU HSI-SHENG says, "Who can imitate the Way of Heaven and make it the Way of Humankind by taking what one has in abundance and giving it to those in need? Only those who possess the Way. The *Yiching* [41–42] says, 'To take means to take from the low and give to the high.' And 'to give means to take from the high and give to the low.'"

LI JUNG says, "Although sages perform virtuous deeds, they expect no reward and try to keep their virtue hidden."

SUNG CH'ANG-HSING says, "The skill of the sages is unfathomable and inexhaustible. How could it be revealed?"

When Lao-tzu refers to "the Way of Heaven," he is not simply referring to the sky above but to everything that lives and moves. In lines thirteen and fourteen, I have followed the simpler wording of Mawangtui B and the Suotan edition. Lines sixteen and seventeen also appear in verse 2, and line seventeen in verse 51, though my translation of them differs slightly in each case. For the last line, I have used the briefer Fuyi version. This verse is not present in the Kuotien texts.

78

天下莫柔弱於水。而攻堅強者。莫之能先也。
以其無以易之也。柔之勝剛也。弱之勝強也。
天下莫不知。而莫之能行。故聖人之言云。
受邦之垢。是謂社稷之王。受邦之不祥。
是謂天下之王。正言若反。

Nothing in the world is weaker than water
but against the hard and the strong
nothing outdoes it
for nothing can change it
the soft overcomes the hard
the weak overcomes the strong
this is something everyone knows
but no one is able to practice
thus do sages declare
who accepts a country's disgrace
we call the lord of soil and grain
who accepts a country's misfortune
we call the ruler of all under Heaven
upright words sound upside down

HSUAN-TSUNG says, "The nature of water is to stay low, to not struggle, and to take on the shape of its container. Thus, nothing is weaker. Yet despite such weakness it can bore through rocks. Rocks, however, cannot wear down water."

LI HUNG-FU says, "The soft and the weak do not expect to overcome the hard and the strong. They simply do."

HSI T'UNG says, "You can hit it, but you can't hurt it. You can stab it, but you can't wound it. You can hack it, but you can't cut it. You can light it, but you can't burn it. Nothing in the world can alter this thing we call water."

CHU TI-HUANG says, "We can alter the course and shape of water, but we can't alter its basic nature to descend, by means of which it overcomes the hardest and strongest things."

TS'AO TAO-CH'UNG says, "The reason people know this but don't put this into practice is that they love strength and hate weakness."

SUNG CH'ANG-HSING says, "Spies and traitors, thieves and robbers, people who have no respect for the law, disloyal subjects and unfilial children, these are disgraces. Excessive drought and rain, epidemics and locusts, untimely death, famine and homelessness, ominous plants, and misshapen animals, these are misfortunes."

PO-TSUNG says, "Rivers and swamps contain mud. Mountains and marshes harbor diseases. The most beautiful gem has a flaw. The ruler of a state suffers disgrace. This is the Way of Heaven" (*Tsochuan*: Hsuan.15).

SHUN says, "If I commit an offense, it has nothing to do with my people. If my people commit an offense, the offense rests with me" (*Shuching*: 4C.8).

CHUANG-TZU says, "Everyone wants to be first, while I alone want to be last, which means to endure the world's disgrace" (*Chuangtzu*: 33.5).

MENCIUS says, "If the rulers of a state are not kind, they cannot protect the spirits of the soil and grain" (*Mencius*: 4A.3).

SU CH'E says, "Upright words agree with the Tao and contradict the world. The world considers suffering disgrace shameful and suffering misfortune a calamity."

LI JUNG says, "The world sees disgrace and innocence, fortune and misfortune. The follower of the Tao sees them all as empty."

KAO YEN-TI says, "The last line sums up the meaning of the abstruse phrases that occur throughout the *Taoteching*, such as 'to act without acting.' The words may contradict, but they complement the truth."

In line four, *yi* (change) can also mean "to be easy" (Ho-shang Kung), "to slight" (Li Hung-fu), or "to replace" (Ch'en Ku-ying). In line five, Mawangtui B has *shui* (water) in place of *jou* (soft), in which case *kang* (hard) would be taken to mean "metal." Wu Ch'eng puts the last line at the beginning of the next verse, Yen Tsun combines both verses, and some commentators suggest combining this with verse 43. This verse is not present in the Kuotien texts.

79

和大怨。必有餘怨。
安可以為善。是以聖人執左契。
而不以責於人。故有德司契。
無德司徹。天道無親。
恆與善人。

In resolving a great dispute
a dispute is sure to remain
how can this be good
sages therefore hold the left marker
and make no claim on others
thus the virtuous oversee markers
the virtueless oversee taxes
the Way of Heaven favors no one
but it always helps the good

TE-CH'ING says, "In Lao-tzu's day, whenever the feudal rulers had a dispute, the most powerful lord convened a meeting to resolve it. But the resolution of a great dispute invariably involved a payment. And if the payment was not forthcoming, the dispute continued."

WANG PI says, "If we don't arrange a contract clearly and a dispute results, even using virtuous means to settle it won't restore the injury. Thus, a dispute will remain."

SU CH'E says, "If we content ourselves with trimming the branches and don't pull out the roots, things might look fine on the outside, but not on the inside. Disputes come from delusions, and delusions are the product of our nature. Those who understand their nature encounter no delusions, much less disputes."

HO-SHANG KUNG says, "Murderers are killed, and criminals are punished according to their crime. But those who inflict such punishments offend their own human feelings and involve innocent people as well. If even one person sighs, we offend the Heart of Heaven. How can resolving disputes be considered good?"

CH'ENG HSUAN-YING says, "If someone lets go of both sides but still clings to the middle, how can he be completely good?"

CHENG LIANG-SHU says, "In ancient times, contracts were divided in two. In the state of Ch'u, the creditor kept the left half, and Lao-tzu was from Ch'u. In the central plains, this was reversed, and the creditor kept the right half."

SUNG CH'ANG-HSING says, "Seeking to make peace with others is the Way of Humankind. Not seeking to make peace but letting things make peace by themselves is the Way of Heaven. Despite action and the expenditure of energy, energy and action seldom bring peace. Sages therefore hold the left marker because they rely on nonaction and the subtlety of letting things be."

CHIANG HSI-CH'ANG says, "If one does not make demands of others, disputes cannot arise. If one constantly takes from others, great disputes cannot help but occur."

WANG AN-SHIH says, "Those concerned with taxes cannot avoid making claims on others and thus cannot prevent disputes. This is why they lack virtue."

MENCIUS says, "The rulers of the Hsia dynasty exacted a tribute [kung] on every five acres of land. The rulers of the Shang exacted a share [chu] on every seven acres. The rulers of the Chou exacted a tax [ch'e] on every ten acres. In reality, what was paid was a tithe of 10 percent" (Mencius: 3A.3; see also Lunyu: 12.9).

LU TUNG-PIN says, "Those who are good cultivate themselves. They don't concern themselves with others. Once you concern yourself with others, you have disputes. The good make demands of themselves. They don't make demands of others. The Way of Humankind is selfish. The Way of Heaven is unselfish. It isn't concerned with others. But it is always one with those who are good."

The Way of Heaven always helps the good because the good expect nothing. Hence, they are easily helped. The last two lines were a common saying. In the Shuoyuan: 10.25, they conclude an exhortation to keep still. They also appear in slightly different form in the Shuching and in Ch'u Yuan's Lisao: "High Heaven favors no one / but it helps the virtuous." This verse is not present in the Kuo-tien texts.

80

小國寡民。使有十百人之器。而不用。
使民重死。而不遠徙。有舟輿。無所乘之。
有甲兵。無所陳之。使民復結繩而用之。甘其食。
美其服。安其居。樂其俗。鄰邦相望。
雞狗之聲相聞。民至老死。不相往來。

Imagine a small state with a small population
let there be labor-saving tools
that aren't used
let people consider death
and not move far
let there be boats and carts
but no reason to ride them
let there be armor and weapons
but no reason to employ them
let people return to the use of knots
and be satisfied with their food
and pleased with their clothing
and content with their homes
and happy with their customs
let there be another state so near
people hear its dogs and chickens
but live out their lives
without making a visit

HUANG-TI says, "A great state is *yang*. A small state is *yin*."

SU CH'E says, "Lao-tzu lived during the decline of the Chou, when artifice flourished and customs suffered, and he wished to restore its virtue through doing nothing. Hence, at the end of his book he wishes he had a small state to try this on. But he never got his wish."

YAO NAI says, "In ancient times, states were many and small. In later times, they were few and great. But even if a great state wanted to return to the ancient ways, how could it?"

HO-SHANG KUNG says, "When sages govern great states, they think of them as small states and are frugal in the use of resources. When the people are many, sages think of them as few and are careful not to exhaust them."

HU SHIH says, "With the advance of civilization, the power of technology is used to replace human labor. A cart can carry thousands of pounds, and a boat can carry hundreds of passengers. This is the meaning of 'labor-saving tools'" (*Chung-kuo che-hsueh-shih ta-kang*, p. 64).

WANG AN-SHIH says, "When the people are content with their lot, they don't concern themselves with moving far away or with going to war."

THE *YICHING CHITZU* says, "The earlier rulers used knots in their government. Later sages introduced the use of writing" (B.2).

WU CH'ENG says, "People who are satisfied with their food and pleased with their clothes cherish their lives and don't tempt death. People who are content with their homes and happy with their customs don't move far away. They grow old and die where they were born."

CH'ENG HSUAN-YING says, "They are satisfied with their food because they taste the Tao. They are pleased with their clothing because they are adorned with virtue. They are content with their homes because they are content wherever they are. And they are happy with their customs because they soften the glare of the world."

TS'AO TAO-CH'UNG says, "Those who do their own farming and weaving don't lack food or clothes. They have nothing to give and seek nothing. Why should they visit others?"

Where is this place? In line two, some editions delete *jen* (man) in the compound *shih-pai-jen* (labor-saving). I have followed Yen Tsun, Ho-shang Kung, and the Suotan and Mawangtui texts, all of which include it. This phrase can also be interpreted with or without *jen* to mean "tools of war." But Hu Shih's reading, seconded by Cheng Liang-shu, is, I think, more profound. After line ten, Ssu-ma Ch'ien and the Fuyi edition add: "the goal of perfect rule / and everyone is..." But this appears to be an interpolation. Finally, some editions reverse the order of lines thirteen and fourteen but thereby abandon the rhyme. This verse is not present in the Kuotien texts.

81

利既聖辯信
而以人者言
不與不不不
害人積善美
。。。。。
聖己知美
人愈者言
之多不不
道。博信
。天。。
為之博善
而道者者
不。不不
爭知辯
。。。

True words aren't beautiful
beautiful words aren't true
the good aren't eloquent
the eloquent aren't good
the wise aren't learned
the learned aren't wise
sages accumulate nothing
but the more they do for others
the greater their existence
the more they give to others
the greater their abundance
the Way of Heaven
is to help without harming
the Way of the Sage
is to act without struggling

HUANG-TI says, "There's a word for everything. Words that are harmful we say aren't true" (*Chingfa*: 2).

TE-CH'ING says, "At the beginning of this book, Lao-tzu says the Tao can't be put into words. But are its 5,000-odd characters not words? Lao-tzu waits until the last verse to explain this. He tells us that though the Tao itself includes no words, by means of words it can be revealed—but only by words that come from the heart."

SU CH'E says, "What is true is real but nothing more. Hence, it isn't beautiful. What is beautiful is pleasing to look at but nothing more. Hence, it isn't true. Those who focus on goodness don't try to be eloquent. And those who focus on eloquence aren't good. Those who have one thing that links everything together have no need of learning. Those who keep learning don't understand the Tao. The sage holds on to the one and accumulates nothing."

HO-SHANG KUNG says, "True words are simple and not beautiful. The good cultivate the Tao, not the arts. The wise know the Tao, not information. Sages accumulate virtue, not wealth. They give their wealth to the poor and use their virtue to teach the unwise. And like the sun or moon, they never stop shining."

CHUANG-TZU says, "When Lao Tan and Yin Hsi heard of people who considered accumulation as deficiency, they were delighted" (*Chuangtzu*: 33.5). Lao Tan was Lao-tzu's name, and Yin Hsi was the man to whom he transmitted the *Taoteching*.

SUNG CH'ANG-HSING says, "People only worry that their own existence and abundance are insufficient. They don't realize that helping and giving to others does them no harm but benefits themselves instead."

TS'AO TAO-CH'UNG says, "The wealth that comes from giving generously is inexhaustible. The power that arises from not accumulating is boundless."

WU CH'ENG says, "Help is the opposite of harm. Wherever there is help, there must be harm. But when Heaven helps, it doesn't harm, because it helps without helping. Action is the start of struggle. Wherever there is action, there must be struggle. But when sages act, they don't struggle, because they act without acting."

CHIAO HUNG says, "The previous 5,000 words all explain 'the Tao of not accumulating,' what Buddhists call 'nonattachment.' Those who empty their mind on the last two lines will grasp most of Lao-tzu's text."

WANG CHEN says, "The last line summarizes the entire 5,000 words of the previous eighty verses. It doesn't focus on action or inaction but simply on action that doesn't involve struggle."

At the beginning and at the end of the *Taoteching*, Lao-tzu reminds us not to become attached to the words. Let the words go. Have a cup of tea. In lines three and four, the Fuyi edition adds *yen* (words). In the Mawangtui texts, lines three and four are inverted with lines five and six. I haven't used either of these variants, nor have I accepted the variation of the penultimate line introduced by Mawangtui B and the Suotan edition, both of which have *jen* (man) in place of *sheng-jen* (sage). This would result in "the Way of Humankind," which does appear in verse 77, but in a pejorative sense. This verse is not present in the Kuotien texts.

GLOSSARY

—

In addition to proper names and Chinese terms, the following list includes the names and dates of all commentators in the preceding pages along with the titles of texts from which I have quoted selected passages. As in my other books, the romanization system I have used is a modified version of the Wade-Giles. However, in this glossary I have also added the Pin-yin spelling for those more familiar with that system, which was originally developed during China's Great Leap Forward and whose quirks (namely, its use of *x*'s, *z*'s, and *q*'s) were intended to help Russian speakers.

CHANG TAO-LING / ZHANG DAOLING / 張道陵 (A.D. 34–157). Patriarch of the Way of Celestial Masters, the earliest known Taoist movement, which emphasized physical and moral training along with spiritual cultivation. His commentary was lost until a partial copy, including verses 3 through 37, was found in the Tunhuang Caves: s.6825. *Lao-tzu hsiang-erh-chu.*

CHANKUOTSE / ZHANGUOZE / 戰國策 Collection of narratives, some historical, some fictional, based on the events of the Warring States Period (403–221 B.C.). Compiled by Liu Hsiang (ca. 79–6 B.C.) and reedited by later scholars.

CHAO CHIH-CHIEN / ZHAO ZHIJIAN / 趙志堅 Quoted by Chiao Hung.

CH'EN KU-YING / CHEN GUYING / 陳鼓應 (B. 1935). Classical scholar and philosopher who has taught in Taipei and Beijing and annoyed authorities in both places with his outspokenness. *Lao-tzu chu-yi chi-p'ing-chieh.*

CH'ENG CHU / CHENG ZHU / 程俱 (1078–1144). Scholar-official and fearless critic of government policies. *Lao-tzu-lun.*

CH'ENG HSUAN-YING / CHENG XUANYING / 成玄英 (FL. 647–663). Taoist master and proponent of using an eclectic approach to explain the teachings of

Lao-tzu. His commentary was recently reedited from portions found in the Taoist canon and in the Tunhuang Caves: S.2517. It reflects the influence of Chuang-tzu along with Buddhist Sanlun and Tientai teachings and was required reading for Taoists seeking ordination during the T'ang dynasty. *Lao-tzu-shu.*

CHENG LIANG-SHU / ZHENG LIANGSHU / 鄭良樹 (B. 1940). Classical scholar and a leading authority on the Mawangtui texts. His presentation of differences between the Mawangtui and other editions appears in *Ta-lu tsa-chih* vols. 54–59 (April 1977–October 1979). His study of Tunhuang copies of the *Taoteching* is also excellent: *Lao-tzu lun-chi.*

CHIANG HSI-CH'ANG / JIANG XICHANG / 蔣錫昌 (PUBL. 1937). *Lao-tzu chiao-chieh.*

CH'IANG SSU-CH'I / CHIANG SIQI / 強思齊 (FL. 920). Taoist master of the former Shu dynasty (Szechuan province) during the Five Dynasties period. His edition is invaluable for its preservation of the comments of Li Jung, Ch'eng Hsuan-ying, and Yen Tsun, as well as those of Hsuan-tsung and Ho-shang Kung. *Tao-te-chen-ching hsuan-te-tsuan-shun.*

CHIAO HUNG / JIAO HONG / 焦紘 (1541–1620). Noted compiler of bibliographic works. His 1587 edition of the *Taoteching* includes his own occasional comments as well as selected commentaries of mostly Sung dynasty authors, notably Su Ch'e, Lu Hui-ch'ing, and Li Hsi-chai. It remains one of the most useful such compilations. *Lao-tzu-yi.*

CHIEH / JIE / 桀 (D. 1766 B.C.) and CHOU / ZHOU / 紂 (D. 1122 B.C.). Tyrants whose reigns concluded the Hsia and Shang dynasties, respectively.

CHINGFU / JINGFU / 景福 Inscription of the *Taoteching* carved in the second year of the Chingfu period (893) at Lunghsing Temple in Yichou, southwest of Beijing.

CHINGLUNG / JINGLONG / 景龍 Inscription of the *Taoteching* carved in the second year of the Chinglung period (708) also at Yichou's Lunghsing Temple. Authorities in charge of the temple's former site have no idea what happened to these two steles, though several elderly village women told me both were moved south to another county in the same province. My guess is that they are in the archives of the Hopei Provincial Museum in Shihchiachuang. A third *Taoteching* stele, carved in 738, is the lone survivor of Lunghsing Temple's collection of ancient inscriptions.

CHINJENMING / JINRENMING / 金人銘 An inscription that Confucius reports seeing on the back of a metal statue whose mouth was papered over. The statue, he says, was at the entrance to an early Chou dynasty shrine to Houchi, the God of Crops. (See *Kungtzu Chiayu:* 11.) A copy of the inscription currently stands near the entrance to the Duke of Chou's shrine in Confucius' hometown of Chufu.

CHU CH'IEN-CHIH / ZHU QIANZHI / 朱謙之 (1899–1972). Classical scholar and teacher of philosophy and history. His edition of the *Taoteching* presents variants, rhymes, and usages along with his own comments. *Lao-tzu chiao-shih.*

CHU TI-HUANG / ZHU DIHUANG / 朱蒂煌 (1885–1941). Ch'ing dynasty official and early revolutionary. After fleeing China, he returned to devote himself to Buddhism and philosophy.

CH'U YUAN / QU YUAN / 屈原 (340–278 B.C.). China's first great poet and author of the *Lisao.* His suicide in the Milo River is celebrated on the fifth day of the fifth moon as Poet's Day and marked by dragon-boat races to save his body from the water dragons and fishes.

CHUANG-TZU / ZHUANGZI / 莊子 (369–286 B.C.). After Lao-tzu, the greatest of the early Taoist philosophers. The work that bears his name contains some of the most imaginative examples of early Chinese writing and includes numerous quotes from the *Taoteching.* The work was added to by later writers and edited into its present form by Kuo Hsiang (d. 312).

CHUNGYUNG / ZHONGYONG / 中庸 (*DOCTRINE OF THE MEAN*). Attributed to Tzu-ssu, the grandson of Confucius. It forms part of a larger work known as the *Lichi,* or *Book of Rites.*

CONFUCIUS / 孔夫子 (551–479 B.C.). China's most revered teacher of doctrines emphasizing the harmony of human relations. His teachings, along with those of certain disciples, were compiled into the *Lunyu* (*Analects*), the *Chungyung* (*Doctrine of the Mean*), and the *Tahsueh* (*Great Learning*) and until recently formed the basis of moral education in China.

DUKE AI / 哀公 (FL. 5TH C. B.C.). Ruler of the state of Lu and interlocutor of *Lunyu:* 12.9.

DUKE WEN OF CHIN / JIN / 晉文公 (FL. 7TH C. B.C.). Ruler of the state of Chin and hegemon of the central states.

FAN YING-YUAN / FAN YINGYUAN / 范應元 (FL. 1240–1269). One of the first scholars to examine variations in pronunciation and wording in the *Taoteching*. *Lao-tzu tao-te-ching ku-pen-chi-chu*.

FIVE EMPERORS / 五帝 According to the lineage established by China's early historian Ssu-ma Ch'ien, they included Shao Hao (ca. 27th c. B.C.), Chuan Hsu (ca. 26th c. B.C.), Ti K'u (ca. 25th c. B.C.), Yao (ca. 24th c. B.C.), and Shun (ca. 23rd c. B.C.).

FU HSI / FU XI / 伏羲 (CA. 3500 B.C.). Sage ruler of ancient times and the reputed inventor of the system of hexagrams on which the *Yiching* is based.

FUYI / 傅奕 Copy of the *Taoteching* that came to light in 574 near the town of Hsuchou in the grave of one of the concubines of Hsiang Yu. Although the date of his concubine's death is unknown, Hsiang Yu died in 202 B.C. Along with the Mawangtui texts, which date from the same period, this constitutes one of the earliest known copies. Fu Yi (555–639) was a court astrologer and outspoken opponent of Buddhist monasticism who published the text with his own commentary. Subsequent editions suggest Fu Yi made some minor changes involving grammatical particles but did not otherwise alter the text. *Fu-yi chiao-ting ku-pen-lao-tzu*.

HAN FEI / 韓非 (D. 233 B.C.). Student of the Confucian philosopher Hsun-tzu. His collection of rhetoric and antecdotes, known as the *Hanfeitzu*, is noted for its legalist philosophy. Chapters 20 and 21 consist of quotes from the *Taoteching* and include commentaries on verses 38, 46, 50, 53, 54, 58, 59, 60, and 67. Although Han Fei often misconstrues phrases to support his own ideas, his is the earliest known commentary.

HANKU / HANGU PASS / 函谷關 A seventeen-kilometer defile through the loess plateau on the border between Honan and Shensi provinces. Lao-tzu reportedly conveyed to Yin Hsi, the Warden of the Pass, the text that makes up the *Taoteching*.

HO-SHANG KUNG / HESHANG GONG / 河上公 (D. CA. 159 B.C.). Taoist master who lived in a hut beside the Yellow River—hence his name, which means Master Riverside. His commentary emphasizes Taoist yoga and was reportedly composed at the request of Emperor Wen (r. 179–156 B.C.). It ranks next to Wang Pi's in popularity. Some scholars think it was compiled as late as the third or fourth century A.D. by members of the Taoist lineage that included Ko Hung (283–343). There is at least one English translation: Eduard Erkes, Artibus Asiae (Switzerland), 1950. *Lao-tzu-chu*.

HOUHANSHU / 後漢書 (*HISTORY OF THE LATTER HAN DYNASTY*). Compiled by Fan Yeh (398–445) for the period A.D. 25–220.

HSI T'UNG / XI TONG / 奚侗 (1876–1936). Official and classical scholar known for his commentaries on the philosophical texts of the Warring States Period (403–221 B.C.). *Lao-tzu chi-chieh.*

HSIN TU-TZU / XIN DUZI / 心都子 Interlocutor in *Liehtzu*: 8.25.

HSISHENGCHING / *XISHENGJING* 西升經 (*BOOK OF THE WESTERN ASCENSION*). Taoist work apparently composed during the first centuries of the Christian era. It is one of several texts that recount Lao-tzu's reappearance in India following his transmission of the *Taoteching* to Yin Hsi.

HSU YUNG-CHANG / XU YONGZHANG / 許永璋 (PUBL. 1992). Hsu's commentary, which took forty years to compile, is prefaced by a thorough and wide-ranging discussion of the *Taoteching* as poetry. *Lao-tzu shih-hsueh yu-chou.*

HSUAN-TSUNG / XUANZONG / 玄宗 (R. 712–762). One of China's more famous emperors, he was also a skilled poet and calligrapher and was deeply interested in Taoism as well as Buddhism. I have quoted from his own commentary, written in 732, as well as from another commentary compiled under his direction that expands on his earlier effort. *Yu-chu tao-te-chen-ching* and *Yu-chih tao-te-chen-ching-shu.*

HSUEH HUI / XUE HUI / 薛蕙 (1489–1541). Official, classical scholar, and student of the occult. His work on the *Taoteching* is notable for its critical review of previous commentaries. *Lao-tzu chi-chieh* and *Lao-tzu k'ao-yi.*

HSUN-TZU / XUNZI / 荀子 (FL. 300–240 B.C.). Teacher of Han Fei as well as Li Ssu, the First Emperor's infamous prime minister. He is considered the third of the great Confucian philosophers, after Confucius and Mencius. However, his rationalism is often at odds with the idealism of his predecessors. His teachings are contained in a book of essays that bears his name.

HU SHIH / HU SHI / 胡適 (1891–1962). Student of John Dewey and leader of China's New Culture Movement that helped establish vernacular Chinese as a legitimate form of literary expression. *Chung-kuo che-hsueh-shih ta-kang.*

HUAI-NAN-TZU / HUAINANZI / 淮南子 (D. 122 B.C.), A.K.A. LIU AN / 劉安. He was the grandson of Liu Pang, the first Han emperor. He was a devoted Taoist, although his search for the elixir of immortality was prematurely interrupted when he was accused of plotting to seize the throne and was forced to commit suicide. The book named after him is a collection of treatises on mostly Taoist themes written by a group of scholars at his court.

HUANG MAO-TS'AI / HUANG MAOCAI / 黃茂村 (FL. 1174–1190). Scholar and military official. *Lao-tzu-chieh.*

HUANG YUAN-CHI / HUANG YUANJI / 黃元吉 (FL. 1820–1874). Taoist master famous for his sermons and oral expositions of Taoist texts. His commentary, which he dictated to a disciple, focuses on internal yoga as well as on points in common between the teachings of Lao-tzu and Confucius. *Tao-te-ching ching-yi.*

HUANG-TI / HUANGDI / 黃帝 (27TH C. B.C.). Known as the Yellow Emperor, he was the leader of the confederation of tribes that established their hegemony along the Yellow River. Thus, he was considered the patriarch of Chinese civilization. When excavators opened the Mawangtui tombs, they also found four previously unknown texts attributed to him: *Chingfa, Shihtaching, Cheng,* and *Taoyuan.*

HUANGTI NEICHING / HUANGDI NEIJING / 黃帝內經 (INTERNAL TREATISE OF THE YELLOW EMPEROR). Earliest known text on Chinese medicine. It records conversations between the Yellow Emperor and his court physician, Ch'i Po. What appears to be the long-lost *External Treatise* was also found in the Mawangtui tombs.

HUHSIEN / HUXIAN / 苦縣 Established as a prefecture during the Chou dynasty, it was at first part of the state of Ch'en and later part of the state of Ch'u. According to Ssu-ma Ch'ien, Lao-tzu was born in the village of Chujen, just outside the prefectural seat. A series of ostentatious shrines now mark the location of his old home.

HUI-TSUNG / HUIZONG / 徽宗 (R. 1101–1125). Sung dynasty emperor and one of China's greatest calligraphers and patrons of the arts. His commentary was finished in 1118, shortly before he was taken captive by nomad invaders. *Yu-chieh tao-te-chen-ching.*

JEN CHI-YU / REN JIYU / 任繼愈 (B. 1916). Professor of religion and philosophy at Beijing University. His many publications include an English translation of the *Taoteching. Lao-tzu che-hsueh t'ao-lun-chi.*

JEN FA-JUNG / REN FARONG / 任法融 (B. 1930). Director of the Taoist Association of China and abbot of Loukuantai, the Taoist center where Lao-tzu reportedly wrote the *Taoteching.* Master Jen's is the only commentary I know of by a Taoist priest subsequent to the Cultural Revolution. *Tao-te-ching shih-yi.*

KAO HENG / GAO HENG / 高亨 (1900–?). Classical scholar and advocate of using grammatical analysis to elucidate textual difficulties in the *Taoteching*. Many of his insights have been borne out by the texts discovered at Mawang-tui. *Lao-tzu cheng-ku.*

KAO YEN-TI / GAO YENDI / 高延第 (1823–1886). Classical scholar and member of the Hanlin Academy. In addition to providing several unique interpretations of his own, Kao's commentary cites passages of the *Taoteching* that appear in other ancient texts. *Lao-tzu cheng-yi.*

KING HSIANG / XIANG OF LIANG / 梁襄王 (FL. 4TH C. B.C.). Ruler of the small state of Liang (now Kaifeng) and son of King Hui.

KU HSI-CH'OU / GU XICHOU / 顧錫疇 (FL. 1600–1630). Scholar-official. His is one of several commentaries incorrectly attributed to the T'ang dynasty Taoist, Lu Tung-pin. *Tao-te-ching-chieh.*

KUAN LUNG-FENG / GUAN LONGFENG / 關龍蓬 (CA. 1800 B.C.). Prime minister during the reign of Emperor Chieh, last emperor of the Hsia dynasty, who had Kuan killed for his unwelcome advice.

KUAN-TZU / GUANZI / 管子 (D. 645 B.C.). Prime minister of the state of Ch'i. The voluminous work that bears his name more likely incorporates the views of the Chi-hsia Academy that flourished in the Ch'i capital at about the same time.

KUMARAJIVA / 鳩摩羅什 (344–413). Native of the Silk Road kingdom of Kucha and greatest of all translators of Buddhist scriptures into Chinese. *Lao-tzu-chu.*

KUO YEN / GUO YEN / 郭偃 (FL. 7TH C. B.C.). Chief minister of the state of Chin during the reign of Duke Wen.

KUOTIEN / GUODIAN / 郭店 Name of the village, near the city of Chingmen in Hupei province, where fragments of the *Taoteching* were found in 1993. The Kuo-tien copies were found in the tomb of a tutor to the crown prince of the ancient state of Ch'u and were divided into three bundles (A, B, and C). The calligraphy in each bundle is different from the others, as is the selection of verses. Taken together, they constitute less than 40 percent of the text, but given their approximate date, 300 B.C., they constitute its earliest known version.

KUOYU / GUOYU / 國語 (*DIALOGUES OF THE STATES*). Like the *Tsochuan*, with which it overlaps and shares much material, this is a compilation of Chou dynasty history and fictional narrative focusing primarily on the period 770–464 B.C. Traditionally, but erroneously, attributed to Tso Ch'iu-ming.

KUSHIHYUAN / *GUSHIYUAN* / 古詩原 Anthology of pre–T'ang dynasty poetry compiled by Shen Te-ch'ien (1673–1769) and published in 1719.

LI HSI-CHAI / LI XIZHAI / 李息齋 (FL. 1167). Taoist master, practitioner of Taoist yoga, and noted *Yiching* scholar. His commentary extends Lao-tzu's teachings to the state as well as the individual. *Tao-te-chen-ching yi-chieh.*

LI HUNG-FU / LI HONGFU / 李宏甫 (FL. 1574). His commentary can be found appended to a reissue of Su Ch'e's commentary. In his preface, he says the differences between Confucius and Lao-tzu are no more significant than the preference for wheat in North China and rice in the South. *Lao-tzu-chieh.*

LI JUNG / LI RONG / 李榮 (FL. 670). Taoist master and proponent of the Chunghsuan (Double Darkness) approach to the truth, which first uses darkness to break through the dialectic of darkness and light then renounces darkness as well. His commentary has been recently reedited from portions that survive in the Taoist canon as well as from several Tunhuang copies. *Tao-te-chen-ching-chu.*

LI YUEH / LI YUE / 李約 (FL. 683). Military official, accomplished poet, calligrapher, and painter of the plum tree. He viewed the Confucian classics as no more than leaves and branches and the *Taoteching* as the root. *Tao-te-chen-ching hsin-chu.*

LICHI / *LIJI* / 禮記 (*BOOK OF RITES*). Anthology of Confucian writings, including the *Chungyung* and the *Tahsueh*. It was first put together around the second century B.C. and was further edited by Tai Te and his cousin during the following century.

LIEH-TZU / LIEZI / 列子 (FL. 4TH C. BC). Taoist master about whom we know nothing other than that he could ride the wind. The book that bears his name was probably the work of his disciples and later generations of Taoists. The present version dates from the fifth century A.D.

LIN HSI-YI / LIN XIYI / 林希逸 (FL. 1234–1260). Scholar-official who produced commentaries to a number of classics. His commentary on the *Taoteching* is noted for its clarity. *Lao-tzu k'ou-yi.*

LIU CH'EN-WENG / LIU CHENWENG 劉辰翁 (1232–1297). Poet and essayist. He held several official posts but spent most of his life in obscurity, if not seclusion. *Lao-tzu tao-te-ching p'ing-tien.*

LIU CHING / LIU JING / 劉涇 (FL. 1074). Recognized for his literary talent by Wang An-shih, he was given several minor posts but failed to advance due to his fondness for argument. *Lao-tzu-chu.*

LIU CHUNG-P'ING / LIU ZHONGPING / 劉仲平 (FL. 1060). Official and member of Wang An-shih's reform clique. *Lao-tzu-chu.*

LIU PANG / LIU BANG / 劉邦 (247–195 B.C.). Helped overthrow the Ch'in dynasty and became the first emperor of the Han.

LIU SHIH-LI / LIU SHILI / 劉師立 (FL. 1200). *Lao-tzu-chieh-chieh.*

LIU SHIH-P'EI / LIU SHIPEI / 劉師培 (1884–1919). Adds to the work of Wang Nien-sun and others in locating ancient usages of the *Taoteching.* *Lao-tzu-chiao-pu.*

LO CHEN-YU / LO ZHENYU / 羅振玉 (1866–1940). Archaeologist, educator, bibliographer, agronomist, adviser to the last emperor, and among the first scholars to study the Tunhuang copies of the *Taoteching.* *Tao-te-ching k'ao-yi* and *Tun-huang-pen-lao-tzu yi-ts'an-chuan.*

LU HSI-SHENG /LU XISHENG / 陸希聲 (FL. 890). High official and scholar known for his wide learning. His commentary reflects the view that Lao-tzu and Confucius were the spiritual heirs of Fu Hsi (ca. 3500 B.C.), with Lao-tzu emphasizing the *yin* and Confucius the *yang* aspects of the Way of Heaven. *Tao-te-chen-ching-chuan.*

LU HUI-CH'ING /LU HUIQING / 呂惠卿 (1031–1111). Gifted writer selected by Wang An-shih to help draft his reform proposals. His commentary, presented to the emperor in 1078, is quoted at length by Chiao Hung. *Tao-te-chen-ching-chuan.*

LU NUNG-SHIH / LU NONGSHI / 陸農師 (1042–1102). High official and scholar known for his knowledge of ritual. His commentary makes extensive use of quotes from the *Liehtzu* and *Chuangtzu. Lao-tzu-chu.*

LU TUNG-PIN / LU DONGBIN / 呂洞賓 (FL. 845). Leader of Taoism's legendary Eight Immortals and author of a number of Taoist works, including *Secret of the Golden Flower.* Several commentaries have been attributed to him. I have used the *Tao-te-ching shih-yi.*

LUSHIH CHUNCHIU / LUSHI QUNQIU / 呂氏春秋 (*THE SPRING AND AUTUMN ANNALS OF MR. LU*). Commissioned by Lu Pei-wei (d. 235 B.C.), this was probably the first Chinese text written with a unified plan. It purported to contain all that anyone needed to know of the world and was Taoist in conception. Not to be confused with *The Spring and Autumn Annals of Master Yen* or with *The Spring and Autumn Annals* written in the state of Lu and attributed to Confucius.

MA HSU-LUN / MA XULUN / 馬敘倫 (1884–1970). Minister of Education, member of several legislative bodies, and classical scholar. One of the first to suggest rearranging passages of the *Taoteching* to remedy inconsistencies, which he thought were the result of inadvertent shuffling of the wooden strips on which the text was first written. *Lao-tzu chiao-ku.*

MAWANGTUI / MAWANGDUI / 馬王堆 Suburb of Changsha, the capital of Hunan province, it is the site of several Han dynasty graves that were excavated in 1973 and 1974. Among the contents of one of the graves were two copies of the *Taoteching* written on silk. Although the grave was sealed in 168 B.C., the presence or absence of certain characters proscribed after the onset of the Han dynasty suggests that Text A was copied before 206 B.C. and Text B was copied between 206 and 194 B.C. Along with the Fuyi text, and the subsequently unearthed Kuotien texts, they constitute our earliest copies of the *Taoteching*. One noteworthy difference in the Mawangtui texts is their reordering of several verses and the placement of the second half of the text first. However, no other edition has been found that follows suit.

MENCIUS / 孟子 (390–305 B.C.). Ranked with Confucius and Hsun-tzu as the foremost teachers of the philosophy known as Confucianism. He studied with Confucius' grandson Tzu-ssu. The work that bears his name records his conversations with his disciples and various rulers of his day.

MING T'AI-TSU / MING TAIZU / 明太祖 (1328–1398). Grew up in a family of destitute farmers, became a Buddhist monk, joined the rebellion against the Mongols (who had occupied the throne since 1278), and founded the Ming dynasty (1368–1644). His commentary, which he wrote without the help of tutors, was completed in 1374. *Tao-te-chen-ching yu-chu.*

MO-TZU / MOZI / 墨子 (FL. 5TH C. B.C.). Philosopher whose arguments in favor of universal love and against costly funerals put him at odds with the Confucian school, especially Mencius and Hsun-tzu. The work that bears his name was apparently composed after his death by his disciples, who themselves betray differences of opinion concerning their master's views.

MOU-TZU / MOUZI / 牟子 (FL. 3RD C.) High official and author of the *Lihuolun*, the earliest known work that addresses the conflicts arising from Buddhist practice and Chinese tradition.

PAO-TING / BAODING / 庖丁 Knife-wielding cook of *Chuangtzu*: 3.2.

PI KAN / BI GAN / 比干 (FL. 1150 B.C.). Adviser to the last emperor of the Shang dynasty, who had him killed for his too-frank counsel.

PI YUAN / BI YUAN / 畢沅 (1730–1797). Prominent scholar-official with interests in history, philology, and geography. *Lao-tzu tao-te-ching k'ao-yi.*

PO-TSUNG / 伯宗 (FL. 8TH C. B.C.). Minister at the court of Chin. His views are reported in the *Tsochuan*: Hsuan.15.

SHANHAICHING / SHANHAIJING / 山海經 (BOOK OF MOUNTAINS AND WATERS). Shaman's guide to China's mountains and rivers. Attributed to Yu the Great (fl. 2200 B.C.), it was edited into its present form by Liu Hsin (ca. 50 B.C.–A.D. 23). A reliable English translation was published by Taiwan's National Institute for Compilation and Translation in 1985.

SHAO JUO-YU / SHAO RUOYU / 邵若愚 (FL. 1135–1170). *Tao-te-chen-ching chih-chieh.*

SHEN NUNG / SHEN NONG / 神農 (28TH C. B.C.). Legendary ruler of China's prehistoric period. He is venerated as the father of agriculture and herbal medicine in China.

SHIHCHING / SHIJING / 詩經 (BOOK OF SONGS). Collection of some 300 poems from China's earliest historical period, between the twelfth and seventh centuries B.C. Arranged by style and region, it was reportedly compiled by Confucius from a larger corpus of over 3,000 poems. It remained an essential part of traditional education until the twentieth century. There are half a dozen English translations.

SHUCHING / SHUJING / 書經 (BOOK OF DOCUMENTS). Collection of memorials from China's earliest historical periods: the Hsia, Shang, and Chou dynasties. Reputedly edited by Confucius, there are two versions, one of which contains twenty-eight chapters and which most scholars think is genuine, and one with an additional twenty-two chapters of debatable authenticity. Translated into English by James Legge (1815–1897).

SHUN / 舜 (CA. 2250–2150 B.C.). Early sage ruler noted for his filial piety and noninterference in public affairs.

SHUOWEN / 說文 Greatest of China's early etymological dictionaries. It was compiled and first published by Hsu Shen in A.D. 121 and revised and updated with new materials in the T'ang, Sung, and Ch'ing dynasties.

SHUOYUAN / 說苑 Collection of moral tales and political discourses. Attributed to Liu Hsiang (ca. 79–6 B.C.), who also compiled the *Chankuotse*.

SSU-MA CH'IEN / SIMA QIAN / 司馬遷 (145–85 B.C.). Authored with his father, Ssu-ma T'an, the first comprehensive history of China. His biography of Lao-tzu (*Shihchi* [*Records of the Historian*]: 63) constitutes the earliest known record of the Taoist patriarch. There are several English translations.

SSU-MA KUANG / SIMA GUANG / 司馬光 (1019–1086). One of the most famous writers and political figures of the Sung dynasty and adversary of Wang An-shih. His multivolume history of China remains one of the most thorough treatments of China's past up through the T'ang dynasty. His commentary interprets Lao-tzu's text using Confucian terminology and neo-Confucian concepts. *Tao-te-chen-ching-lun.*

SU CH'E / SU CHE / 蘇轍 (1039–1112). He, his father, and his brother are counted among the eight great prose writers of the T'ang and Sung dynasties. Although his commentary reflects his own neo-Confucian sympathies, it is also treasured by Buddhists and Taoists. *Tao-te-chen-ching-chu.*

SUICHOU / SUIZHOU / 遂州 Location in Hupei province where an inscription of the *Taoteching* was carved during the T'ang dynasty at the town's Lung-hsing Temple. Not dated.

SUNG CH'ANG-HSING / SONG CHANGXING / 宋常星 (FL. 1700). Taoist master and seventh patriarch of the Dragon Gate sect of the Golden Lotus lineage. His commentary on the *Taoteching* was a favorite of Emperor K'ang-hsi (r. 1662–1722). *Tao-te-ching chiang-yi.*

SUN-TZU / XUNZI 孫子 (FL. 512 B.C.). Master of military tactics and strategy. His *Pingfa* (*Art of War*) has been much studied and admired ever since it came to the attention of King Ho Lu of the state of Wu, who subsequently became Sun's patron.

SUOTAN / SUODAN / 索統 Partial copy of the *Taoteching*, including verses 51 through 81, found in the Tunhuang Caves. It was copied on paper in A.D. 270 by

Suo Tan, a Tunhuang native famous for his prognostication of dreams. Although it was not included in early Tunhuang catalogues, it has been verified and recopied by Yeh Chien-ting and Huang Pin-hung. Formerly in the collection of Li Mu-chai, it is currently in the possession of Chang Chun.

SWEET DEW / 甘露 Name for the saliva produced during meditation by pressing the tongue against the roof of the mouth. An essential element in the creation of a pure body capable of transcending death.

TAHSUEH / DAXUE / 大學 (GREAT LEARNING). One of the Confucian classics. It was later included as part of the *Lichi* (*Book of Rites*). Some scholars attribute its composition to Confucius' disciple Tseng-tzu, while others think it was written by the Sage's grandson, Tzu-ssu.

TE-CH'ING / DEQING / 德清 (1546–1623). One of the greatest Buddhist writers of the Ming dynasty and responsible for revitalizing the practice of Zen in China. His commentaries on Lao-tzu and Chuang-tzu are among the best ever written and are used by Taoists as well as Buddhists. *Lao-tzu tao-te-ching-chieh.*

THREE SOVEREIGNS / 三皇 Fu Hsi (ca. 3500 B.C.), Shen Nung (ca. 2800–2700 B.C.), and Huang-ti (ca. 2700–2600 B.C.).

TS'AO TAO-CH'UNG / CAO DAOCHONG / 曹道沖 (FL. SUNG DYNASTY: 960–1278). Taoist nun about whom I have found no other information. *Lao-tzu-chu.*

TSENG-TZU / ZENGZI / 曾子 (B. 505 B.C.). Disciple of Confucius and author of the *Hsiaoching* (*Book of Piety*). His views are also quoted at length in the *Lunyu* and the *Tahsueh.*

TSOCHUAN / ZUOZHUAN / 左傳 (ANNALS OF TSO). First comprehensive account of the major political events of the Spring and Autumn Periods (722–481 B.C.). It was compiled during the fourth century B.C. by Tso Ch'iu-ming, about whom we know nothing else.

TU ER-WEI / DU ERWEI / 杜而未 (1913–1987). Scholar of Chinese religion and comparative mythology and proponent of the view that Taoism had its origin in the worship of the moon. *Lao-tzu-te-yueh-shen tsung-chiao.*

TU TAO-CHIEN / DU DAOJIAN / 杜道堅 (FL. 1264–1306). Taoist master and author of commentaries to a number of Taoist classics. His *Taoteching* commentary makes extensive use of quotes from the Confucian classics. *Tao-te-hsuan-ching yuan-chih.*

TUNG SSU-CHING / DONG SIJING / 董思靖 (FL. 1246–1257). Taoist master and compiler of Taoist texts in the Lingpao tradition. His commentary includes extensive quotes from T'ang and Sung dynasty commentators as well as his own comments. *Tao-te-chen-ching chi-chieh*.

TUNHUANG / DUNHUANG / 敦煌 China's westernmost outpost on the Silk Road over two thousand years ago and later the location of Buddhist devotional caves carved into a nearby hillside from the fourth through the fourteenth centuries. At the end of the nineteenth century, a Taoist caretaker opened a sealed side-room in one of the caves and found more than 30,000 manuscripts, most of which dated from the eighth through the eleventh centuries. From 1907 onward, he began selling these manuscripts to collectors, and the majority ended up in the national archives of France and England. Although most were Buddhist sutras, they included at least sixty copies of various portions of the *Taoteching*.

TZU-SSU / ZISI / 子思 (D. 483 B.C.). Grandson of Confucius and author of the *Chungyung*.

WANG AN-SHIH / WANG ANSHI / 王安石 (1021–1086). One of China's most famous prime ministers. His attempt to introduce sweeping reforms directed against merchants and landowners galvanized Chinese intellectuals into a debate that continues to this day. He was also one of China's great poets and prose writers. His commentary has been reedited from scattered sources by Yen Ling-feng. *Lao-tzu-chu*.

WANG CHEN / WANG ZHEN / 王真 (FL. 809). T'ang dynasty general and student of the *Taoteching*. His commentary, which he personally presented to Emperor Hsiuan Tsung, remains unique for its display of pacifist sympathies by a military official. *Tao-te-ching lun-ping yao-yi-shu*.

WANG NIEN-SUN / WANG NIANSUN / 王念孫 (1744–1832). Distinguished philologist whose analysis of grammatical particles used in ancient texts is unrivaled. His approach is also unique in not taking characters at their face value but in viewing them as possible homophones. *Lao-tzu tsa-chih*.

WANG P'ANG / WANG PANG / 王雱 (1044–1076). Brilliant scholar, writer, and son of Wang An-shih. His commentary, written in 1070, was "lost" until Yen Ling-feng reedited it from various sources. *Lao-tzu-chu*.

WANG PI / WANG BI / 王弼 (226–249). Famous for the quickness of his mind as well as the breadth of his learning. He grew up with one of the best private libraries of his time. Although he died of a sudden illness at the age of twenty-four, he was among the first to discuss Taoism as metaphysics rather than religion. As a result, his commentary has been preferred over that of Ho-shang Kung by Confucian scholars. At least two English translations exist: Paul Lin, University of Michigan Center for Chinese Studies, 1977; Ariane Rump, University of Hawaii Press, 1979. *Lao-tzu-chu.*

WANG TAO / WANG DAO / 王道 (1476–1532). Incorporates Confucian interpretations in his commentary. *Lao-tzu-yi.*

WANG WU-CHIU / WANG WUJIU / 王無咎 (FL. 1056). Scholar-official. He gave up a promising official career in order to devote himself to studying and teaching. *Lao-tzu-yi.*

WEI YUAN / 魏源 (1794–1856). Classicist, historian, geographer, and admired administrator. While his own views are insightful, his commentary consists largely in selections from Chiao Hung's earlier edition. *Lao-tzu pen-yi.*

WEN-TZU / WENZI / 文子 (FL. 5TH C. B.C.). Taoist recluse and teacher of Fan Li, prime minister of the state of Yueh. According to the *Hanshu* (*History of the Han Dynasty*), he was a disciple of Lao-tzu and a contemporary of Confucius. The book that bears his name is attributed to his disciples.

WU CH'ENG / WU CHENG / 吳澄 (1249–1333). One of the great prose writers of the Yuan dynasty, surpassed only by his student Yu Chi (1272–1348). His commentary shows exceptional originality and provides unique background information. It is also noted for its division of the text into sixty-eight verses. *Tao-te-chen-ching-chu.*

YANG / 陽 The bright side, the male, the strong.

YANG HSIUNG / YANG XIUNG / 揚雄 (53 B.C.–A.D. 18). Gifted philosopher and writer of courtly odes. Known for his view that man is neither good nor bad by nature but wholly subject to his environment. A number of his odes are preserved in the literary anthology known as the *Wenhsuan.* The *Fayen* contains his philosophical maxims.

YAO NAI / 姚鼐 (1732–1815). One of the most famous literary figures of the Ch'ing dynasty and advocate of writing in the style of ancient prose. His anthology of ancient literary models, *Kuwentzu Leitsuan,* has had a great influence on writers and remains in use. *Lao-tzu chang-chu.*

YELLOW EMPEROR / 黃帝 (CA. 2700–2600 B.C.). Patriarch of Chinese culture. He was also among the earliest known practitioners of Taoist yoga and other hygienic arts.

YEN FU / 嚴復 (1853–1921). Naval officer, scholar, and the first Chinese commentator to use Western philosophical concepts in interpreting Lao-tzu. *Lao-tzu tao-te-ching p'ing-tien.*

YEN LING-FENG / YEN LINGFENG / 嚴靈峰 (B. 1910). Classical scholar and specialist in *Taoteching* studies. In addition to his own books on the subject, he republished most of the surviving commentaries in his monumental *Wu-ch'iu-pei-chai lao-tzu chi-ch'eng,* including a number of "lost" commentaries that he reconstructed from diverse sources. *Lao-tzu chang-chu hsin-pien.*

YEN TSUN / YEN ZUN / 嚴遵 (FL. 53–24 B.C.). Urban recluse of Chengtu. He supported himself as a fortune-teller and spent his remaining time reading and pondering the *Taoteching.* The lengthy commentaries that he produced are sometimes quite profound but more often obscure, and those that survive are incomplete. He divides the text into seventy-two verses. *Tao-te-ching chih-kuei.*

YENTIEHLUN / YENTIELUN / 鹽鐵論 (DISCOURSE ON IRON AND SALT). Record of debates on government policies and other problems of the day compiled by Huan K'uan (fl. 73 B.C.).

YICHING / YIJING / 易經 (BOOK OF CHANGES). Ancient manual of divination based on a system of hexagrams invented by Fu Hsi (ca. 3500 B.C.) with judgments attributed to Duke Wen and the Duke of Chou (c. 1200–1100 B.C.), and commentaries added some 600 years later, reportedly by Confucius.

YICHING CHITZU / YIJING JIZI / 易經繫辭 (APPENDED JUDGMENTS ON THE BOOK OF CHANGES). Attributed to Duke Wen.

YIN / 陰 The dark side, the female, the weak.

YIN HSI / YIN XI / 尹喜 (FL. 6TH C. B.C.). Taoist astronomer who met Lao-tzu at Hanku Pass and to whom Lao-tzu subsequently conveyed the *Taoteching.* Several works have been attributed to him, though those that survive are probably by later Taoists.

YIN WEN / 尹文 (350–284 B.C.). Eclectic philosopher of the state of Ch'i and author of a book of discourses that bears his name.

YU JUO / YU RUO 有若 (FL. 5TH C. B.C.). Disciple of Confucius known for his resemblance to the sage as well as for his love of antiquity. After Confucius' death, many of his disciples wanted to render to Yu Juo the same observances they had conferred on Confucius. But this was opposed by Tseng-tzu.

YUNCHI CHICHIEN / YUNJI QIJIAN / 雲笈七籤 Anthology of Taoist writings editing by Chang Chun-fang (fl. 1017–1021). One of the most influential such compilations, it is also called the *Shorter Taoist Canon.*

ABOUT THE TRANSLATOR

Bill Porter assumes the pen name Red Pine for his translations. He was born in Los Angeles in 1943, grew up in the Idaho Panhandle, served a tour of duty in the U.S. Army (1964–67), graduated from the University of California with a degree in anthropology in 1970, and attended graduate school at Columbia University. Uninspired by the prospect of an academic career, he dropped out of Columbia in 1972 and moved to a Buddhist monastery in Taiwan. After four years with the monks and nuns, he struck out on his own and eventually found work at English-language radio stations in Taiwan and Hong Kong, where he produced over a thousand programs about his travels in China. In 1993 he returned to America with his family and has lived ever since in Port Townsend, Washington. His most recent publications are *Zen Baggage*, an account of a pilgrimage to sites associated with the beginning of Zen in China, and *In Such Hard Times: The Poetry of Wei Ying-wu*, a translation of one of China's greatest poets. He is currently working on a translation of the *Lankavatara Sutra*.

The Chinese character for poetry is made up of two parts: "word" and "temple" (or originally, as Red Pine notes, "from the heart"). It also serves as pressmark for Copper Canyon Press.

Since 1972, Copper Canyon Press has fostered the work of emerging, established, and world-renowned poets for an expanding audience. The Press thrives with the generous patronage of readers, writers, booksellers, librarians, teachers, students, and funders—everyone who shares the belief that poetry is vital to language and living.

Major funding has been provided by:

Amazon.com

Anonymous

Beroz Ferrell & The Point, LLC

Cynthia Hartwig and Tom Booster

Golden Lasso, LLC

Lannan Foundation

National Endowment for the Arts

Cynthia Lovelace Sears and Frank Buxton

Washington State Arts Commission

For information and catalogs:

COPPER CANYON PRESS
Post Office Box 271
Port Townsend, Washington 98368
360-385-4925
www.coppercanyonpress.org

Copper Canyon Press acknowledges the following donors
and thanks them for their extraordinary support
for *Lao-tzu's Taoteching:*

Amazon.com

Joseph Bednarik and Liesl Slabaugh

Janet and Leslie Cox

Stanton Reed Koch

David Dietrich

Paul Dietrich

Dot Dolese

Thomas Dolese

Imants E. and Elsa E. Golts

Chris Higashi

Kathie Werner

Jim Westall

This book is set in Minion, designed for digital composition by Robert Slimbach
in 1989. Minion is a neohumanist face, a contemporary typeface retaining
elements of the pen-drawn letterforms developed during the Renaissance.
Display type is set in Classica, designed by Thierry Puyfoulhoux.
Book design and composition by Valerie Brewster, Scribe Typography.
Chinese typesetting by Pristine Communications in Taipei, Taiwan.
Printed on archival-quality paper at McNaughton & Gunn, Inc.